Discoveries

Lord, Open Our Eyes That We May See.
2 Kings 6:17

Dan Harless

GOSPEL ADVOCATE COMPANY
Nashville, Tennessee
Copyright© 1982

ISBN 0-89225-207-3

Foreword

Over the past ten years, at the request of the elders, a weekly ramble has appeared on the front page of THE HILLSBORO HERALD, bulletin of the Hillsboro Church of Christ, Nashville, Tennessee. Free rein has been given the writer and he has touched numerous themes from a wide variety of sources, including personal experiences. Naturally, he has dipped into the greatest of all books, the Bible. This sampling covers some of the many things that have piqued the curiosity and concern of the writer. He passes them on for your consideration and delectation.

Nashville, Tennessee
January, 1982

TABLE OF CONTENTS

Introduction

The ability to write with imagination and power is by no means common in our day. Writers there are in great abundance but, as has been aptly observed of after-dinner speakers, "Only one in a thousand qualifies as such but the other nine hundred ninety-nine think they do!" Remarkably, failures in this field of creative effort often result from extremes of both over and under preparation. Men and women of broad mental powers, endowed by nature with superior intellects and students totally dedicated to their work not infrequently live and breathe the rarified air of profundity so long and so much that they have lost interest in the mundane matters of the world ever with us, while others, content with mediocrity both in thought and in effort, are without ability to interest and excite us with their shallow and often inept productions.

Of neither of these categories is Dan Harless, prince of essayists and author of this remarkable collection of timely observations which he has drawn out from a life-time of study and seasoned with a rich measure of practical Christianity which he so beautifully reflects both in teaching and in life. His themes are simple, practical, stimulating, often witty and always thought-provoking and they range over the whole spectrum of man's eventful and exciting journey from the cradle to the grave.

So great is his craftmanship with words of our rich and wonderful English heritage and so incisively does he write that one often experiences the thrilling sensation of actually having been transported into the scenes he so vividly and skillfully depicts. More than fourscore essays appear in this volume and the subject-matter is of the greatest variety, yet there is an over-all-unity pervading these paragraphs which keeps the reader evermore reminded that it is not by bread alone we survive and that there is a divinity which shapes our ends roughhew them however much we may. The delightful themes which are included in this rich collection will stimulate, arouse, excite, motivate and sometimes amuse and all of them will make us immeasurably better from having allowed them to enter our heads and hearts.

—GUY N. WOODS, Editor
GOSPEL ADVOCATE
Nashville, Tennessee

1
Discoveries

Ever since man walked on the moon this scribe, who admittedly was confident such a feat would never be accomplished, has noted a widespread tendency to accept without question some rather grandiose claims for the future. Yet if all were to come true it should be noted there remains a fearsome gap between man's technology and his spirituality. Moreover, with all his brilliance, from time to time there are inevitable slips in calculation as well as prophecy. On the credit side, with the exception of proponents of various evolutionary theories who remain adamant in support of their theories in spite of a lack of evidence, scientists seem ready and willing to admit error. Some preachers would do well to "go thou and do likewise."

Recently we came across an item having to do with a discovery by three scientists. They found that a generally accepted rule (Hubble's Constant, the number astronomers have been using to figure distance between objects in space) is not to be relied upon. According to their findings the constant, which is the ratio of speed to distance, should be almost twice as large as previously thought. This, it was stated, means "the age of the universe is but 9 billion years instead of 15 billion."

We are reminded of that old story about a sleepy youngster in science class who was jolted wide awake by a statement of his teacher. The boy asked excitedly, "When did you say the earth will explode?" The teacher said he thought it would be in about 50 million years. Greatly relieved, the boy said, "You scared me; I thought you said 15 million."

This great universe holds many mysteries and with each new finding, it seems, new and greater mysteries arise. While

1

we are constantly amazed at the discoveries of science, we would that all these brilliant and dedicated men and women might make the ultimate discovery. It is to be found in the opening lines of the greatest of all books: "In the beginning (whenever that may have been) God (First Cause, Prime Mover, Omnipotent One, Heavenly Father) created the heavens and the earth."

And with that marvelous discovery, would that all might accept the revelation of the Holy Spirit that "Christ Jesus came into the world to save sinners."

2
Life's Imponderables

No subject has produced more discussion, with more varied conclusions, than the problem of human suffering. Both the believer and the skeptic are preoccupied with this matter. Both are in agreement with Eliphaz that "man is born to trouble as the sparks fly upward" and with Job that "man that is born of a woman, is of few days and full of trouble" (Job 5:7; 14:1).

There is no escape from suffering, be it a momentary toothache or the stark realization that terminal cancer is gnawing away at one's vitals. And, of course, there is suffering of the spirit as well as the flesh. There comes, for example, the pain of separation and loneliness. Then there is for some the utter bewilderment that comes with the departure of children, or husband or wife, from righteousness—in spite of years of seeming exemplary living.

We read recently of a rock singer whose life style embraced alcohol and drugs, accompanied by a wild promiscuity suggestive of an animal rather than a human being. The report reveals her wasted life came to an end as a result of an overdose of drugs. The thought comes to mind that this was to be expected for the "way of the transgressor is hard" (Prov. 13:15). But this is not the problem. The problem has to do with suffering that comes to the upright, to those who fear God and endeavor to obey His commands, and to the innocent child who knows nothing of sin.

God's natural laws are unremitting, as are His spiritual laws. A wonder drug is thought to be a universal panacea. Later its disastrous side effects are discovered. A child wanders into the path of an oncoming car and is crushed. A virus that knows not the mind and heart of its victim brings agony and death. When blows fall we are left to wonder. But the Christian's wonder is not the dull despair of the unbeliever. He refuses to believe that suffering is the end of hope. Instead, though he may not understand, he accepts the evil with the good. He may even achieve a majesty of outlook such as moved Job to cry. "Though he slay me, yet will I trust him" (Job 13:15).

For every godly man or woman subjected to peril and suffering there seems to be a thousand ungodly people who prosper. The Psalmist said, "I was envious at the arrogant, when I saw the prosperity of the wicked. For there are no pangs in their death; but their strength is firm. They are not in trouble as other men; neither are they plagued like other men." He wonders about himself: "Surely in vain have I cleansed my heart." But later, upon mature consideration, he realizes the wicked are doomed to destruction and that it is good "to draw near unto God" for refuge is to be found only in the Lord Jehovah (Psalm 73:3-5, 13, 28). As with the Psalmist, so with the apostle Paul who, living in hope, looked for "the glorious appearing of the Great God and our Savior Jesus Christ" (Titus 2:13).

3

Observations in response to the oft-heard statement that things are no different now than in days gone by

A cartoon in the *Saturday Review* pictured a savage sitting in front of his grass hut. A boy, presumably his son, is walking toward the jungle. The dusky savage calls out, "Be careful, it's a city out there." We are impressed, following a visit to the Big Apple, with the appropriateness of the cartoon. Hundreds of once proud buildings have fallen into decay. Some have been gutted by fire; others appear to have been bombed. There are no window panes. We were informed that owners, saddled with ever-rising taxes and rent ceilings, have simply abandoned their properties. Incredible urban blight is the result. Even worse is moral decay, accompanied inevitably by violence, thievery, misuse of narcotics, and extreme permissiveness.

We remember a visit some years ago when we walked down Fifth Avenue to 42nd Street, thence to Times Square and the Great White Way. It was most pleasant. How different now. Adult (what a misnomer!) book stores line the streets. Theatres vie with each other in advertising indecent movies and live shows. A depraved moral sickness engulfs the area. How unlike the days when "Abie's Irish Rose," "Smilin' Thru," "Life With Father," and other delightful offerings beckoned.

Before we throw in the towel, however, it would be well to remember that New York is still a world capital, filled with cultural advantages, and a challenge to the church of our

4

Lord. It would be equally well to remember that the apostle Paul faced even worse conditions in Ephesus. A thousand courtesans occupied the infamous temple of Diana. Carnality reigned. Yet we find him saying, ". . . A great door and effectual is opened unto me" (1 Cor. 16:9).

Satan is powerful, undeniably so, whether on Broadway in New York or on lower Broad Street in Nashville—but our Lord is all-powerful (Matt. 28:18; Rev. 1:8, 17-18).

4

Joy to the World

Some time ago the well-known author, Vance Havner, told of a great meeting in which many hearts were touched. One man went home after the meeting still turned on by all he had seen and heard. In his prayer that night he rehearsed the thrilling scene in great detail. In a burst of enthusiasm he wound up his recital, saying, "Lord, I wish you could have been there."

Absurd as the foregoing may sound, it must be admitted that there are all too many who seemingly cannot grasp the fact that God is everywhere and that our Lord has promised to be with his own "even unto the end of the world."

The church is now in position to present the saving gospel to more people over a wider area in less time than at any period in history. This in spite of the fact that some who sing of standing on the promises are merely sitting on the premises.

There is a growing opposition to liberalism and cultism as well as toward long-established institutions that are unsupported by biblical precepts. For example, a recent report reveals that priests are leaving the priesthood at the rate of one thousand per year and nuns are leaving at about three times that rate.

While Madalyn O'Hair contends that "prayer is useless because there is no heaven or hell, no Jesus Christ and no God," there are increasing numbers everywhere who are enlightened, having tasted of the heavenly gift, made partakers of the Holy Spirit, tasted the good word of God, and the powers of the age to come (Heb. 6:4-5).

The outlook of unbelievers is consistently morose and hateful. Not so with the Lord's people. It is the Master's will that his followers be joyous. He would have his own to "be of good cheer" (John 16:33), a condition that flourishes even amid hardship and trial. With the apostle Paul they are capable of rejoicing always (1 Thess. 5:16). Conversely, the unbeliever remains cheerless and bitter though surrounded by material blessings.

The victorious Christ arose from the dead, the firstfruits of all who sleep (1 Cor. 15:20). His resurrection is the Christian's hope (1 Cor. 15:23).

Joy to the world, the Lord is come (Luke 2:10-11). Joy to the world, He is risen (Matt. 28:6). Joy to the world, we shall see Him when He comes again (Acts 1:11). Joy to the world, we shall be glorified with Him (Rom. 8:17).

5

Vicarious Suffering

Philosophers have pondered, theologians have theorized, Bible scholars have searched, and disciples of Christ since the beginning have stood amazed before this mystery of the ages. We read in the opening pages of the Bible. "I will put enmity between thee and the woman, and between thy seed and her seed: he shall bruise thy head and thou shalt bruise his heel" (Gen. 3:15). Christ is the "seed of the woman," born of a virgin, who would bruise the head of the serpent. But in bruising the serpent's head he would also be bruised—"for our iniquities."

We may never know the full answer as to why Christ was crucified. The important thing is that we accept it. When Paul preached that magnificent sermon to the Athenians he mentioned the resurrection of Christ from the dead. Many began to mock the apostle at this point. They regarded the central theme of Christianity as mere foolishness. Yet the reality of the suffering of Christ is revealed with terrible clarity—in Gethsemane and on Golgotha. He sweat as it were great drops of blood. Then on the cross He gave His blood, a sin offering for the world. We do not see the need for constantly attempting to analyze the mystery. The lowest aborigine can receive the full benefit of His sacrifice, provided he believes and obeys the Christ (Heb. 5:8, 9).

When you stop to think of the matter, vicarious suffering is required for man to live in this world just as it is required for him to be redeemed. A condition of birth is the suffering of a mother (Gen. 3:16). As for the land in which we live, the freedoms we enjoy, the luxuries that are now ours—all have come about as a result of the physical and mental efforts, the anguish and sacrifice of others. Is it too much to accept the need for vicarious suffering whereby the soul of man might live forever?

"We have been sanctified through the offering of the body of Jesus Christ once for all" (Heb. 10:10).

6

Sanctification

Where livest thou? In pleasure of the world?
Or in that realm whence Satan's darts are hurled?
Choose now to follow with the sons of God;
Far better this than where the great have trod.

7

In his great Sermon on the Mount Jesus proclaimed, "Ye therefore shall be perfect, as your heavenly Father is perfect." Yet there is a false humility which causes many to disclaim any possibility of perfection. Consequently, we hear it said with dulling repetitiveness, "Nobody's perfect," a statement often used to justify further imperfections.

Actually, it is true that nobody is perfect. The Bible is in accord with this finding. However, the same Bible would have all men strive with all the power of their being for perfection. Imperfection, our own or our neighbor's, is not a mask behind which we are privileged to hide. Our lives must be spent in a constant struggle to achieve the highest good—and God being for us, the possibilities for spiritual achievement are illimitable.

The word "sanctification" is lightly esteemed in our day. It means simply to be set apart. The Christian has been set apart from the world and the church is God's called out. "Ye were washed, but ye were sanctified, but ye were justified in the name of the Lord Jesus Christ, and in the Spirit of our God" (1 Cor. 6:11).

Because Christians are the called out, sanctified people, the apostle Paul warned, "Be not fashioned according to this world: but be ye transformed by the renewing of your mind, that ye may prove what is the good and acceptable and perfect will of God" (Rom. 12:2).

Sanctification is not to be confused with the sanctimony of the hypocrite. Sanctification is the ideal prescribed by our Lord.

7

Identity

It is always fascinating to watch the struggles of a man who does not know who he is or where he is bound. The subject of amnesia, therefore, has become a favorite theme among novelists and playwrights. Perhaps this fascination stems from the fact that we find little or no difficulty in putting ourselves in the victim's place, sharing his frustrations and anxieties.

Scientists in general and geneticists in particular are enamored with the discoveries of the past few years. They tell us that their probings have revealed that mysterious code inherent in all living organisms whereby life forms are governed. We are informed further that deoxyribonucleic acid (DNA) is a living computer that holds the secret of molecular and biological structure and behavior. Consequently, the units of DNA have been on the receiving end of exhaustive studies.

However, the answer to man's yearning for identity is not to be found in the laboratory. A cure for cancer, for which the world waits longingly, would not relieve all groanings of spirit and agonies of soul. It is a matter of record that even when unbelievers' irreligion is blatantly paraded, wistful dreams and longings refuse to die; instead, they become more pronounced.

"What is man, that Thou art mindful of him?" (Psalm 8:4). For one thing, our rightful, God-given heritage includes partaking of the divine nature (2 Pet. 1:4). This means, of course, that we are more than mere creatures of the dust. "Jehovah God formed man of the dust of the ground," but it is equally true that He "breathed into his nostrils the breath of life; and man became a living soul" (Gen. 2:7). The ultimate identity failure comes in a refusal to claim kinship with God. "Behold what manner of love the Father hath bestowed upon us, that we should be called the children of God; and such we are . . ." (1 John 3:1).

8
Ataraxia

Everybody talkin' about peace of mind ain't findin' it—
cause jus about everybody lookin' in the wrong place.

The foregoing paraphrase of a well-known spiritual may
serve to open a door to introspection. The most of us are prone
to imagine that a few simple changes in our lives would
guarantee peace of mind. We are rather confident that all
would be well if
income were to exceed outgo (page Mr. Micawber), if
a little weight could be lost, if
a little weight could be gained, if
income taxes were abolished, if
children were more submissive, if
parents were more lenient, if
friends were more understanding, if
health were better, if, IF, *IF* . . .

Alas, "man that is born of woman is of few days and full of
trouble" (Job 14:1). Even Longfellow, that wonderful pur-
veyor of good cheer, admitted that

> Into each life some rain must fall,
> Some days must be dark and dreary.

The answer to man's longing for peace of mind lies in that
unquenchable spark called hope. Man is saved, among other
things, by hope (Rom. 8:24). Hope, leading to peace of mind,
may be engendered by a baby's happy smile, by a word of
encouragement in time of need, by a knowledge of the reliability of the stars in their courses, and by all things great and
small that attest the goodness and power of God. Above all,
there is hope and peace of mind to be found in our heavenly
Father's promise to His obedient children of life everlasting
(Rev. 22:14).

9
Reverence for the Word

The doorposts of many Jewish homes tell a story. On the right side of the entrance is a little case on which the Hebrew word *shaddai* (almighty) appears. Inside the case is a mezuzah which consists of a small parchment scroll containing two paragraphs from the Book of Deuteronomy (the Torah). In one paragraph, chapter 6:4-9, are the familiar words, "Hear, O Israel, the Lord our God, the Lord is One. And thou shalt love the Lord thy God with all thy heart, with all thy soul, and with all thy might." When Jesus was asked by a scribe which commandment was first of all, he quoted this very passage, adding, "The second is this, Thou shalt love thy neighbor as thyself" (Mark 12:28-31). The passage continues, "These words which I command thee this day shall be upon thy heart . . . and thou shalt write them upon the doorposts of thy house and upon thy gates."

The second paragraph in the mezuzah, Deuteronomy 11:13-21, outlines rewards for obedience, punishment for disobedience, and the necessity of teaching children the word of God.

In our country and throughout the world there are three differing groups among Jews. There are conservatives who accept the Mosaic law as binding but allow adjustments to changing conditions. There are the reformed who do not accept the Mosaic law in its entirety or the interpretations of the law found in the Talmud. Moral values are stressed rather than ritual and ceremony. Then there are the orthodox who accept as binding the Mosaic law and the authoritative rabbinical interpretations in the Talmud.

In the Christian world there are also three differing groups. There are liberals who do not object to "going beyond that which is written." There are those of universalist leanings whose beliefs are so nebulous as to allow them to reject

11

God's word and Christ as God's Son. Finally, there are those who insist upon a "thus saith the Lord" in all things pertaining to faith and practice.

It would be well to remember, as we read the stringent commands of God to the children of Israel, that the apostle Paul, who describes himself as a "Hebrew of the Hebrews" (Phil. 3:5), informs us that the history of God's chosen people was "written for our admonition, upon whom the ends of the ages are come" (1 Cor. 10:11).

10
Poetry and the Bible

Poetry is more lasting than military might. Through countless wars, now mostly forgotten, great poetry has endured, becoming even more lustrous with the passing of years.

In Keats' "Endymion," written 160 years ago, are the familiar lines, "A thing of beauty is a joy forever: Its loveliness increases; it will never pass into nothingness. . . ." To be sure, never is a long, long time.

Some 200 years before "Endymion" Shakespeare produced the lovely sonnet that begins, "Shall I compare thee to a summer's day?" Go back 300 years before Shakespeare and find Chaucer writing of a Morning in May in which "The busy larke, messager of daye, Salueth in hire song the morwe graye." The spelling is unlike our own but the beauty and imagery are there.

Yet these are but voices of yesterday compared to the ancients whose inspired words are found on the pages of the Bible. Some 2300 years before Chaucer, David wrote the words that have been quoted in every generation since: "The Lord is my shepherd; I shall not want. . . ." Look 500 years beyond David and find those exquisite words recorded by

12

Moses, "The Lord bless thee, and keep thee: The Lord make his face shine upon thee, and be gracious unto thee: The Lord lift up his countenance upon thee, and give thee peace."

We are confident, though in some far off age the words of the great poets shall have been lost and unremembered, that the word of God will continue—till the end of time. His word is forever. Therefore, it is for man to read and heed.

Down through 25 centuries comes the plea of Jeremiah: "O earth, earth, earth, hear the word of the Lord!"

11

"Never Man So Spake"

The libraries of the civilized world contain words of wisdom, words that enrich and ennoble the mind of man. Lovers of great books are thrilled by these enduring records. But of all great books it is a certainty that none is comparable to the gospel of our Lord Jesus Christ for therein is that which is able to save the eternal soul (James 1:21), the power of God unto salvation (Rom. 1:16).

Jesus was never at a loss for words. He was never thrown off guard. He never met a problem too big or too complex for him to solve. He never encountered a man of superior mentality. He could and did silence formidable opponents with a single question (Luke 20:4). "My words," he said, "shall not pass away" (Luke 21:33). Yet there are vast areas where his word is unknown or disregarded. More frightening than nuclear devastation are the barren deserts of mind and heart that result from ignorance of the words of our Lord.

The multitudes who thronged Jesus wherever he went were astonished at his teaching and the fact that he "taught them as one having authority, and not as their scribes" (Matt. 7:29). They were right for he laid claim to supreme authority (Matt. 28:18) and he easily demonstrated his right to so ex-

13

alted a claim. He was calm under pressure, merciful to the despairing, and compassionate toward the sick and suffering. His actions were never out of harmony with his words. He practiced what he preached. Luke tells us his record has to do with "all that Jesus began both to *do* and to *teach*"(Acts 1:1). There was a time when men came to take him. When they returned empty-handed they excused themselves on the grounds that "never man so spake" (John 7:46).

Honesty demands obedience to our Lord's commands. It is one thing to hear his words; it is quite another to obey. Obedience is the great test of love. "If a man love me, he will keep my word" (John 14:23). At the close of his magnificent Sermon on the Mount the Master settled for all time the necessity of obedience. "Everyone therefore that heareth these words of mine, and doeth them, shall be likened unto a wise man, who built his house upon the rock: and the rain descended, and the floods came, and the winds blew, and beat upon that house; and it fell not: for it was founded upon the rock. And everyone that heareth these words of mine, and doeth them not, shall be likened unto a foolish man, who built his house upon the sand: and the rain descended, and the floods came, and the winds blew, and smote upon that house: and it fell: and great was the fall thereof" (Matt. 7:24-27).

12
Taking Christ Seriously

Repentance is a change in the controlling will that leads to reformation of life and character. That repentance must occur in the life of the alien sinner is clearly taught in the New Testament. Jesus reveals that man's choice is to repent or perish (Luke 13:3). Peter and Paul are equally insistent regarding the necessity of repentance (Acts 2:38; 17:30).

Repentance is required of the erring Christian as well as the alien. Simon the Magician was a baptized believer who, when he had sinned, was commanded, "Repent . . . of this thy wickedness, and pray the Lord if perhaps the thought of thy heart shall be forgiven thee" (Acts 8:22). In his epistle addressed to Christians, John wrote, "If we confess our sins, he is faithful and righteous to forgive us our sins, and to cleanse us from all unrighteousness" (1 John 1:9). Likewise, Peter's exhortation to Christians reads, "The Lord is not slack concerning his promise . . . but is longsuffering to us-ward, not willing that any should perish, but that all should come to repentance" (2 Pet. 3:9).

Confession by alien sinner and erring Christian alike is an indication of genuine repentance. The alien confesses Christ to be the Son of God (Rom. 10:9, 10). The erring Christian must confess his sin (1 John 1:9). The denominational world long has misunderstood this plain truth.

Whenever one takes Christ seriously (which includes repentance for all sin, past and present), there comes an inevitable change in that person's life. The misanthrope will begin to love people; the man who found it necessary to lie "if the occasion demanded," becomes a stickler for truth; the libertine centers his thoughts and affections on wholesome pursuits while sublimating the sensual and base. This is not to say the allure of sin disappears but rather that taking Christ seriously will affect one's life, changing and purifying outlook and motives. "As many as received him, to them gave he power to become the sons of God, even to them that believe on his name" (John 1:12).

13
Botany and the Bible

The Bible has much to say about plant life. As is almost universally known, the first sin came about because of fruit that was lovely to look at, good for food, and to be desired because it would make one wise (Gen. 3:6). After the fall, God revealed that the soil would bring forth thorns and thistles. Amateur gardeners as well as farmers are intimately acquainted with these hazards, along with plantains, dandelions, and ubiquitous crab grass. We are also aware of the fact that some of the loveliest of plants are poisonous while some that are unsightly are extremely beneficial as food or medicine.

Jesus calls attention to the beauty of flowers in his great teaching on the futility of worry. "Consider the lilies of the field, how they grow; they toil not, neither do they spin: And yet I say unto you, that even Solomon in all his glory was not arrayed like one of these." Then he adds, "Wherefore, if God so clothe the grass of the field, which today is, and tomorrow is cast into the oven, shall he not much more clothe you, O ye of little faith?" (Matt. 6:28-30).

It is interesting to note that herbs and spices were brought by the wise men when Jesus was born in Bethlehem. Moreover, when he was laid in the tomb by Nicodemus, use was made of a hundred pounds of myrrh and aloes. Then, when Mary Magdalene and others came to the tomb they brought a preparation of spices and ointments (John 19:39; Luke 23:56).

In the first Psalm we find David's simile describing the reward of a righteous man, "He shall be like a tree planted by the rivers of water, that bringeth forth his fruit in his season."

Good deeds are referred to in the Bible as good fruit. Conversely, evil deeds are called bad fruit. In a great passage

16

from the apostle Paul is the significant statement, "The fruit of the Spirit is love, joy, peace, longsuffering, gentleness, goodness, faith, meekness, temperance; against such there is no law" (Gal. 5:22-23).

14
Big Bang vs. First Cause

Robert Jastrow, physicist, astronomer and author, is an agnostic who admits "I keep coming close to the edge of faith, but I never quite make it over." Would that he might read the apostle Paul's statement, "Faith cometh by hearing the word of God." Jastrow takes into consideration a co-worker's opinion that "when a physicist or astronomer begins to write about God, he is over the hill." We question this evaluation as did Dr. Vannevar Bush who, while vice-president of MIT, published his sparkling book, *Science Is Not Enough*. Dr. Bush wrote, "He who follows science alone comes to a barrier beyond which he cannot see. Young men, who will formulate the deep thought of the next generation, should lean on science, for it can teach much. But they should not lean where it does not apply."

Dr. Bush, the father of the modern computer, knew there is an area that cannot be investigated even by the most sophisticated tools of science. Strangely enough, Jastrow, a firm supporter of the "big bang" theory of the birth of the universe, and in spite of his agnosticism, says the scientists' evidence "now supports just what the theologians have been saying all along—there was a First Cause, a force from which everything came." Jastrow says "the galaxies were all in one place about 20 billion years ago." (As with Washington's dealings in dollars, a few billion years more or less don't seem to make much difference.) He insists that in that far off time "the universe exploded and formed stars, planets, and then

17

life." All of this, he says, will eventually dissipate and the universe "will die a cold, lonely death."

The inspired apostle presents a different picture. "The day of the Lord," he says, "will come as a thief; in the which the heavens shall pass away with a great noise, and the elements shall be dissolved with fervent heat, and the earth and the works that are therein shall be burned up" (2 Pet. 3:10). As for the beginning, the only authentic record of that mighty event is found in the opening sentence of the book of Genesis: "In the beginning God created the heavens and the earth."

Agnostics are troubled about their tenuous theories relating to the beginning. Believers are untroubled, resting in the assurance of faith that the First Cause, the Prime Mover, the Creator of all things is Jehovah God, that the heavens are the work of his fingers (Psalm 8:3), and that even the lowliest of his children may approach him through the Savior as their loving heavenly Father. Thanks be to God for his love. Thanks be to God for his Son, in whom we have redemption.

15
"Help Thou Mine Unbelief"

"I shall keep in mind the fact that I am speaking from the grave because I shall be dead when the book issues from the press." Thus speaks Mark Twain in the opening lines of his autobiography, a book that is remarkably humorous, sad, loving, sacrilegious, wrathful, and kind.

Twain's daughter Susy was thirteen when she wrote a biography of her illustrious father. He was deeply moved and after her untimely death he wrote, "As I read it now, after all these years, it is still a king's message to me and brings me the same dear surprise it brought me then—with the pathos added of the thought that the eager hand that scrawled it will not touch mine again."

18

Many hard blows were suffered by Mark Twain during his seventy-five years. It is merely conjecture on our part but we are of the opinion that the hardest blow of all came when he was made to realize the burden he had placed upon his wife Olivia, whom he adored. During a time when she was hard pressed, almost beyond endurance, he suggested that she resort to prayer. She replied, "I cannot pray. Because of what you have taught me I no longer believe in God." Her husband, a man who had brought laughter to the world, took that bitter declaration to his grave.

As death approached, it seems this strange, gifted man wanted to believe. The last words of the autobiography have to do with the death of another daughter: "Now Jean is in her grave! In the grave—if I can believe it. God rest her sweet spirit!" And four months later Mark Twain was dead.

We are reminded of the father of an afflicted child who with tears said to Jesus, "Lord, I believe; help thou mine unbelief" (Mark 9:24). Would that Mark Twain had accepted help from the Master in his time of need.

16

How Faith Comes

On the flyleaf of the paperbound edition of Halley's justly famous *Bible Handbook*, of which more than three million are in print, Dwight L. Moody is quoted as follows: "I prayed for faith, and thought that some day faith would come down and strike me like lightning. But faith did not seem to come. One day I read in the tenth chapter of Romans, 'Now faith cometh by hearing, and hearing by the word of God.' I had closed my Bible, and prayed for faith. I now opened my Bible, and began to study, and faith has been growing ever since."

Would you have faith? Would you strengthen that faith so that it will stand, come what may, through all the days ahead? Then read, study, and meditate upon the holy word of God.

It was the apostle Peter who said, "No prophecy ever came by the will of man but men spake from God, being moved by the Holy Spirit" (2 Pet. 1:21). And Paul expressed it in this manner: "Every scripture inspired of God is also profitable for reproof, for correction, for instruction which is in righteousness: that the man of God may be complete, furnished completely unto every good work" (2 Tim. 3:16-17).

Millions of people read tons of literature on tens of thousands of subjects, every day of the year. The well-known expression, "mountains of paper and rivers of ink," far from being a mere figure of speech, is an actuality. Yet of all the millions of books in the world, there is but one book by which faith comes. No man can afford to remain unsupported by faith in this treacherous world of fear and anxiety.

> How precious is the book divine,
> By inspiration given!
> Bright as a lamp its precepts shine,
> To guide my soul to heaven.

17

Truth, Belief, and Obedience

Excerpt from THE EXISTENCE OF GOD by Thomas Aquinas, 13th century philosopher and theologian: ". . . The existence of truth is self-evident; for whoever denies the existence of truth concedes that truth does not exist. Now, if truth does not exist, then the proposition 'Truth does not exist' is true. But if there is anything true, there must be truth."

Aquinas' argument sneaks up on those in our time who grudgingly admit to the existence of truth but insist that all truth is relative. Our Lord said, "Ye shall know the truth," not relative or nearly so, "and the truth shall make you free." He also said, "Thy word is truth." He once asked, "If I say truth, why do ye not believe me?"

An outstanding teaching of our Savior has to do with the blessings attached to genuine acceptance of his word as opposed to its rejection. In John 3:36 is the statement, "He that *believeth* on the Son hath eternal life; but he that *obeyeth not* the Son shall not see life, but the wrath of God abideth on him."

Note how the words italicized above are used interchangeably. Obedience invariably accompanies belief. Even as his word is truth so he himself is truth (John 14:6) and one must believe on him or be lost. ". . . Except ye believe that I am he, ye shall die in your sins" (John 8:24).

There are many who profess to believe in God and in the Lord Jesus Christ who turn away from certain of his commands, especially from the command to be baptized. Yet failure to obey this command is the strongest possible indication of failure to believe. The believer will obey. This is truth, not almost or nearly so but absolute. The Savior asks, "Why call ye me, Lord, Lord, and do not the things which I say?" (Luke 6:46).

18
Seeing and Hearing Vs. Believing

There has never been a time since the creation when faith was not required by God and needed by man. Fortunately, from the infinitesimal world of the atom to the vast reaches of space, there are impressive indications of a Supreme First Cause. And, in a book that has weathered every attack, instilled hope in every generation, and answered the deepest longings of the soul, there is, for earnest seekers, abundant and enduring cause for faith.

Doubting Thomas said he would not believe unless he could see the print of the nails in the Master's hands. Later, Jesus replied "Because thou hast seen me, thou hast believed: blessed are they that have not seen, and yet have believed" (John 20:29).

Faith is "assurance of things hoped for, a conviction of things not seen" (Heb. 11:1). Paul wrote, "For in hope were we saved: but hope that is seen is not hope" (Rom. 8:24). Yet in another place he speaks of Moses "as seeing him who is invisible" (Heb. 11:27). Verily, this is the essence of faith and hope—achieving the impossible, seeing the invisible, and attaining the unattainable.

Our sense of sight, though it is truly marvelous, is limited to a small amount of light, from the short waves of violet to the long rays of red. Beyond these there are light waves and rays which are invisible to us. As for hearing, there are numbers of sound waves in our world and in the universe that we cannot hear. Although the human ear is a remarkably sensitive instrument, it catches only a small portion of the sound waves that literally fill the atmosphere. The average person has a range from low A to high C, give or take a little. In spite of these obvious limitations, we encounter those who endeavor to bring the infinite down to their finite level. They posit seeing and hearing as absolute requisites to faith. But since we are unable to see and hear light and sound waves that are all about us, why insist on seeing God and hearing God in order to believe? "No man hath seen God at any time" (John 1:18). So says the scripture. So be it!

19

On Praise and Obedience

Throughout what is loosely called Christendom the Bible receives the accolades of countless people—many of whom rarely read and study the book whose praises they sing.

We are reminded of the astronaut who made an author happy when he said, "I was reading your book while we were in orbit—and I couldn't put it down." Later, when the author had time to think about the matter, he was somewhat less happy.

Of all the world's great literature, the highest and noblest of all books, is the Bible. It is the Book of books, the very word of God. The Bible is worthy of all the praise that has been heaped upon it and it is worthy of the unswerving obedience it demands.

There is an air of infallibility about the writers of the Bible, even though many of them were unlearned and ignorant men. They claimed unequivocally to speak from God. We find expressions such as these: "God spake all these words . . ." (Ex. 20:1). "Thus saith Jehovah to his anointed . . ." (Isa. 45:1). "Unto us God revealed them . . ." (1 Cor. 2:10). "No prophecy ever came by the will of man; but men spake from God, being moved by the Holy Spirit" (2 Pet. 1:21). "I make known to you, brethren, as touching the gospel which was preached by me, that it is not after man. For neither did I receive it from man, nor was I taught it, but it came to me through revelation of Jesus Christ" (Gal. 1:11-12).

The Bible has been compared to a great sea—shallow enough at its shore for a child to wade safely, yet so deep and wide as to be far beyond the complete mastery of the strongest swimmers. Fortunately, God's commands can be understood, commands such as this familiar one: "Give diligence to present thyself approved unto God, a workman that needeth not to be ashamed, handling aright the word of truth" (2 Tim. 2:15).

20
Steps

Many years ago Marshall Keeble preached a sermon on the subject, "Five Steps to the Church and Seven Steps to Heaven." In fact he preached it again and again to attentive and responsive audiences throughout the south.

In the course of his sermon Brother Keeble would say, "We have in the church a ladder that Christians climb to heaven. Trouble is, some are tryin' to climb Ladder No. 2 that ain't never climbed Ladder No. 1." Then, with the aid of chart and abundant scripture references for each step, Keeble showed the five steps to the church are hearing, believing, repenting, confessing Christ, and burial with the Lord in baptism. The seven steps to heaven, he said, are virtue, knowledge, temperance, patience, godliness, brotherly-kindness, and love.

In days long gone by, Keeble's sermon was preached by young preachers, black and white. As a result many souls were added to the church of our Lord. Came the day, however, when his "five and seven step religion" was frowned upon, along with the earlier "five finger exercise" of Walter Scott. First principle sermons, it was argued, had been preached to death. It was reasoned further that everybody was familiar with the format and the time had come to go on to other matters.

Admittedly, sermons on "Establishment of the Church," "What Must I Do to be Saved?" "Conversion of Paul," "Conversion of Lydia," "Conversion of the Jailor," etc. had been preached many times over until audiences were pretty well aware of what preachers were going to say next. But was that bad? or was the people's awareness an estimable virtue? Men and women in those days, it must be acknowledged, were able and quite ready to "give answer" to those who asked a reason for their hope (1 Pet. 3:15), nor did they think it necessary to wait to be asked.

24

This is not to say, of course, that there are no knowledge-able people in the church today. However, some time ago considerable space in the papers was devoted to discussions of "The Man OR the Plan," with strong emphasis on the man. Actually, the man, the Lord Jesus Christ, the world's only Redeemer, must be preached; we must also preach his plan of salvation. The true gospel cannot be preached when either man or plan is omitted. And the plan contains certain com-mands of our Lord (call them steps or what you will) that must be obeyed.

21

When Blind Men See

Winfield Kinsey of Annapolis, Maryland, was blind for fifty of his sixty-two years. When he was twelve years old a mishap on his father's farm caused lime to be sprayed directly into his eyes. Kinsey learned to make the best of a difficult situation. He went to school, graduated, was married, and lived a nor-mal life, save for his inability to see.

Recently an ophthalmologist told Kinsey he was confident his sight could be restored by means of a cornea transplant. Kinsey submitted to the operation. When the bandages were removed he saw his wife and two children for the first time. It was a great moment in his life.

The story calls to mind Mark's account of Bartimaeus. When Jesus went out from Jericho with a great host of his followers, Bartimaeus was sitting on the side of the road. When he heard that it was Jesus who was passing by he began to cry out, "Jesus, thou son of David, have mercy on me." The people accompanying our Lord evidently felt that the blind man was sounding a discordant note on an otherwise joyous occasion. He was asked to hold his peace. The blind man had other thoughts on the matter and "he cried out the more a great deal."

Jesus heard his cry and asked, "What wilt thou that I should do unto thee? The blind man said unto him, Rabboni, that I may receive my sight. And Jesus said unto him, Go thy way; thy faith hath made thee whole. And straightway he received his sight, and followed him in the way."

When Bartimaeus opened his eyes, the first thing he saw was the Lord Jesus Christ. As with Bartimaeus so with all whose eyes are opened by "the light of the gospel of the glory of Christ" (2 Cor. 4:4).

22
How Not to Be Saved

The church was established in accordance with the eternal purpose of God (Eph. 3:11) at a fearful cost—the blood of Christ (Acts 20:28). Yet, from the moment of its inception the church has been scorned and castigated by sinful men (Acts 2:13; 2 Tim. 4:3-4).

Of the many familiar objections to the church perhaps the most persistent is that old saw about its being a place wherein hypocrites may be found. Would-be paragons sternly refuse to have anything to do with the church because of their "honesty" and because they "refuse to violate conscience in the matter."

It all sounds noble and virtuous. But suppose we accompany one such despiser of hypocrites on an imaginary cruise down on the beautiful Caribbean. On the second night an explosion rocks the ship and it begins to settle with frightening rapidity. As our man joins a group of passengers boarding a lifeboat we advise him strongly against this sensible procedure.

"But why?" asks the astonished erstwhile foe of the church, "can't you see the ship is sinking?"

"Oh yes, but we also know the lifeboat to which we have been assigned has some hypocrites in it. Surely you will not violate your conscience by escaping in the company of such people."

"Don't be silly. Let go of my arm. I say, get out of my way!" So says the one-time hater of hypocrites. His attitude during a few stressful moments has undergone a remarkable change.

The ship called the world is sinking. We are warned not to love it (1 John 2:15). The church is the lifeboat to which we have been assigned. It is to be saved by our Lord (Eph. 5:23). On the other hand, there is not so much as a shadow of an intimation in the scriptures that one may be saved apart from His church.

23

Fit for the Kingdom

In the popular *Light From Many Lamps* is an account of Dr. A. J. Cronin's trials in the writing of *Hatter's Castle*, the first and most successful of his many books.

The doctor began writing while recuperating from an illness which caused him to drop everything and go away to a quiet little village in Scotland for his health. The book was begun as a pastime to while away long hours spent in seclusion. However, as the book began to take shape Cronin found the demands of concentration to be almost unbearable. He knew nothing of the fine points and technicalities of writing. Plot structure and style were completely foreign to his knowledge and experience.

One day in desperation he snatched up the loose pages of the manuscript and tossed them into the trash can. To celebrate his liberation he walked through the fields to the shore of a lake. There he saw an elderly scotsman with whom he was acquainted. Cronin poured out his story. The old man, though sympathetic, did not approve. He had been trying for ever so long to convert a bog into a pasture. Now, with shovel in hand, he said of his seemingly hopeless task, "Pasture or no pasture, I canna help but dig."

Stung by the implied rebuke, Dr. Cronin returned to the house, retrieved and dried his manuscript which had been exposed to a shower, and then set to work in earnest. About a year later the book was published and soon it became a best seller. Eventually, it was translated into nineteen languages bringing fame and wealth to the author.

There is little to admire in a quitter. Moreover, our Lord will not countenance one. Thus we find Him saying, "No man, having put his hand to the plow, and looking back, is fit for the kingdom of God" (Luke 9:62). And it was the apostle Paul sho said, "Let us not be weary in well-doing: for in due season we shall reap, if we faint not" (Gal. 6:9).

24

Birds, Bombs, a New Year and the Saving Gospel

". . . a bird of the heavens shall carry the voice, and that which hath wings shall tell the matter" (Eccles. 10:20).

Many years ago, in a more peaceful time, we enjoyed a pleasant, leisurely visit to the Minor Bird Sanctuary in Ontario, Canada. Mr. and Mrs. Jack Minor, who loved the beauties of nature, had turned their farm with its lovely lake into a bird sanctuary. Feed was provided by the Minors for migrating ducks, geese, and other birds. The feathered travelers seemed to sense they could break their long journey without fear of being molested. Countless numbers dropped in each year for a rest and a snack.

The Minors caught and banded thousands of birds with a scripture quotation. Hunters returned the bands from far-away places, such as Colombia, South America, three thousand miles from the Minor farm. An Eskimo above the Arctic circle became interested in knowing more about the book from which the quotation had been taken. Responses poured in from all over the western hemisphere.

With a new year before us we are faced with opportunities to preach the word as never before. Yet our hearts are filled with concern as ominous international reports fill the papers and air waves. We are informed of Russian soldiers invading far off Afghanistan. Thus another link is removed from the protective chain once maintained by allies against Soviet aggression. We watch helplessly as a deliberately godless super power seems destined to add a weak and primitive land to its far-flung domain, a land, we add, that knows not Christ. And after this coup perhaps Iran, Iraq, and other nations on whose oil and mineral resources the aggressors have fastened greedy eyes, will be added to the stronghold of Communism.

Of deep concern is the possibility that somewhere a button will be pressed releasing a nuclear device. This would be the signal for the start of World War III, with the threat of incineration for all the great cities of the world. However, we reject the seeming possibility of the world's destruction by man. That cataclysm remains for the mighty hand of God (2 Pet. 3:10).

We are pleased with the wholesome story of the Jack Minors' method of sending forth the word in bits and pieces. However, we are under obligation to teach and preach the whole counsel of God by every available means. We do not know how much time remains. We do know that in order to reap there must be a time of sowing (Matt. 13). We also know that whatsoever we sow, that shall we also reap (Gal. 6:7).

25

Death Sentence

The thirst for power has moved men to the grossest of evil deeds. Their atrocities have blackened the pages of history. The infamous Attila, known to history as the Scourge of God, made the 5th century a time of terror for millions throughout central Europe. But on the eve of what was to have been a crushing invasion of Italy, he died. Genghis Khan, in the early 13th century, with no qualms of conscience, plundered the greater part of Asia. History records that he was "a bold leader and military genius, but one who left few permanent institutions." A century later came Tamerlane, the Earthshaker, from whose fabled Samarkand warriors went out to pillage the entire Oriental world. But at the zenith of his powers the mighty Tamerlane was overtaken by death. In modern times the names of Hitler and Stalin have brought terror to millions. But now these who were so greatly feared are dead. How the mighty are fallen.

The foregoing brings to mind a news item which states there are several hundred people in America who have been sentenced to die. Actually, there are more than four billion human beings who have been sentenced to die. Not one can expect commutation of this fearsome fate for "it is appointed unto men once to die, and after this cometh judgment" (Heb. 9:27).

Someone has said facetiously that anything so universal as death must be a good thing. And yet, certainly, there is an element of truth in the statement for we know that "flesh and blood cannot inherit the kingdom of God" (1 Cor. 15:50). How one lives is of the greatest possible importance. "When a wicked man dieth, his expection shall perish" (Prov. 11:7) but "Precious in the sight of the Lord is the death of his saints" (Psalm 116:15).

26
Clout

Time was when the word *clout* was defined variously as something having to do with a patch, a piece of cloth, an iron plate, the mark used in archery, a blow with the hand and, in baseball, an extra base hit. In recent years, however, the word has taken on new meaning. Clout these days is something or someone with power, prestige, and special abilities. A credit card, for example, is said by its advertisers to have enormous clout, which is to say it is widely accepted in lieu of cash.

Some people strive for clout by falling in line with current styles in dress and behavior. Others assume that clout comes by adopting words and speech patterns that have become popular. Consequently, certain forms of dress, behavior and speech, no matter how weird, are slavishly followed by a great many people.

Since space is limited we shall confine this scriven to a brief discussion of speech. Our mother tongue is a noble language. It is shameful when lazy people, insensitive to nuance and style allow their barbarisms to ride roughshod over the language. Whereas language, admittedly, is subject to change, it is needful for us to be aware that worn phrases and meaningless vogue words *(you know?)* are capable of destroying its beauty and effectiveness.

One can become addicted to the use of expletives which, ordinarily, are crutches. Crutches are for hobbling rather than enhancing. Plain, crisp, unadorned speech is a mark of maturity. Young men and women would do well to mark the words of the apostle Paul: "When I was a child, I spake as a child, I felt as a child, I thought as a child: now that I am become a man I have put away childish things" (1 Cor. 13:11). It was this same apostle, the possessor of an abundance of clout, who said, "Let your speech be always with grace, seasoned with salt, that ye may know how ye ought to answer each one" (Col. 4:6).

There is beauty of life and beauty of speech. One without the other is a ship without a rudder. Consider the prayer of David: "Let the *words of my mouth* and the *meditation of my heart* be acceptable in thy sight, O Jehovah, my rock, and my redeemer" (Psalm 19:14).

27
Standardization

Recently an unknown writer came out in support of standardization as a boon to human pursuits. "Without standards of measurement, there would not only be no commerce, but no science and no industry," he states, and "without standards to guard our safety the world would be a minefield of hazards."

These are safe assumptions. Think what Henry Ford's assembly line did for the automobile industry. Or consider the matter of words. Words are understood only because they are standardized. It is essential that they mean to others what they mean to us. This is the point of difficulty. For example, the word *peace* suggests to the average person a place of untrammeled security and freedom from the ills that beset a frenetic world. With leaders in the Kremlin, however, peace means the absolute subjugation of the entire world under the particular brand of Marxism advocated by the Soviet Union. This is a fearful breakdown in standardization.

In recent years there have been efforts to standardize measurement on a world-wide scale by adoption of the metric system. Much has been said pro and con on the subject. It must be admitted in all fairness that it would be helpful if a measure were adopted that is recognized and accepted the world over.

Great as is our interest in standards that are applied to these varied endeavors, there is an area that is of far greater importance. Obviously, we are thinking in terms of moral and spiritual guidance. There is but one infallible measurement and that, of course, is the word of God. Imagine the result of universal acceptance of the inerrancy of the Bible. Peter, in telling of the origin of the Bible, says "Men spake from God, being moved by the Holy Spirit" (2 Pet. 1:21). Paul says, "All scripture is given by inspiration of God . . ." (2 Tim. 3:16). And Jesus himself says, ". . . Thy word is truth" (John 17:17).

The standardization of God's plan for man's redemption is seen in the fact that the Bible speaks of but one church and one faith rather than a multiplicity of churches and faiths (Eph. 4:4-6). Christ is shown to be the Savior of his church (Eph. 5:23; Col. 1:18) and his gospel is designed for the salvation of mankind (Rom. 1:16). The "unity of the Spirit in the bond of peace" (Eph. 4:3) is achieved only by the acceptance of Christ as "the way, the truth, and the life" (John 14:6).

"There is a way which seemeth right unto a man, but the end thereof are the ways of death" (Prov. 14:12).

28

On Things Great and Small

You've heard, of course, of the fellow who always carried a whistle with which to scare away elephants. To all and sundry attempting to point out the absurdity of such behavior his stock and somewhat edgy reply was, "You don't see any elephants around here do you?"

On the morning of May 16 this scribe could have used such a whistle. Mind you, I didn't see any elephants that morning but it must have been a ponderous pachyderm that kicked me in the chest and then sat on me. My recollection of the events of that day as well as the ensuing week is rather sketchy. The trip to the hospital, with ambulance siren screaming, called to mind Lincoln's story of the man who was tarred, feathered, and ridden out of town on a rail. Quoth he: "Except for the honor I can't say I cared much for the ride."

As a result of emergency treatment the elephant removed his bulk from my chest. Later, in cardiac care, Dr. Ralph Massie's jovial features floated in and out of my consciousness as he issued orders and dispensed his special brand of wit and wisdom. The kindness and concern of doctors, nurses and attendants was remarkable.

After coming face to face with the grim reaper one is prone to place higher values on ordinary, everyday things. There comes a greater appreciation for the sunrise serenade of birds, a meticulous savoring of the exquisite beauty of gems of dew on a spider's web, and delight in the billowing vastness of clouds, whether white and lazy or ominously black and stormy. At night, seated on back yard patio, one senses with David how the heavens declare the glory of God. The radiance of ten thousand times ten thousand suns dotting the far reaches of space proclaim the majesty and limitless power of the Creator. One is humbled by the knowledge that light from some of those blazing stars has traveled trillions of miles across the dark void and through aeons of time, untold light years of time, before reaching this planet on which God has seen fit to place us. And be it remembered that the mighty heavens are but the work of God's fingers (Psalm 8:3).

One feels constrained to shout with the angelic chorus, "Glory to God in the highest, and on earth peace among men in whom He is well pleased," and to echo the adoration of the Psalmist who exhorted, "Let everything that hath breath praise Jehovah" (Luke 2:14; Psalm 150:6).

29

The Case for Atheism

A newspaper item states that "Dial-A-Prayer has a competitor with the arrival of Dial-An-Atheist." The message was introduced by the New York Chapter of the Society of Separationists, also known as American Atheists. It is part of a national group founded, as you might have guessed, by Madalyn O'Hair.

All the fools (Psalm 14:1), some educated, some uneducated, who say there is no God, are perfectly free to do so. They are also free to propagate atheism, as it is being done on a gigantic scale by the Russian government—and by dilettantes in our own richly blessed land. Coercion is not a part of God's plan for the redemption of mankind. Freedom of choice is given to every responsible person.

The word of God has been given that we might know God, accept His sovereignty, believe in His Son, obey His commands, and rejoice in hope. The awesome majesty of God, the Creator of earth and all the universe, is such as to fill the heart of the believer with reverence and fear. Yet, open defiance of God is becoming ever more blatant in a world gone mad with delusions of its own greatness. As with the ancients, "There is no fear of God before their eyes" (Psalm 36:1; Rom. 3:18).

"The fear of Jehovah is the beginning of wisdom" (Psalm 111:10). Solomon said, "Pride and arrogancy, and the evil way, and the perverse mouth, do I hate" (Prov. 8:13). The ultimate arrogance is seen in those who parade their unbelief and attempt to undermine the faith of others.

What worthwhile contributions toward the alleviation of human suffering is being made by atheists? what assistance is offered the destitute? what provisions for the betterment of the human situation? wherein have they endeavored "to see another's profit and work another's gain?" When their ideals (if such they can be called) are adopted by the major portion of

35

our land, the result will be chaos, utter and complete. There is no case for atheism.

Our nation, the greatest the world has ever seen, has been fashioned by the Christian ethic. In time past its moral codes have been imbued with the teaching of the Savior of mankind. Today, however, we face a danger far greater than that posed by Russia. The danger lies in the nation's departure from godliness.

As was true three thousand years ago, "Blessed is the nation whose God is Jehovah" (Psalm 33:12).

30

Awareness

The adage "Know thyself" has come to us from the dim past. It is attributed to various ones including Thales, Socrates, Plato, Cervantes and Pope.

Self-awareness is thought by many to be the summum bonum of human achievement. But it ain't necessarily so. Some there are who are completely aware of their inner compulsions—to which, unfortunately, they give free rein. In so doing they are free of compunction, due to the untimely death of conscience (1 Tim. 4:2). Awareness apart from conscience is extremely dangerous to the individual and a matter of grave concern, in our fear-stricken society, to all who are exposed to uninhibited, unconscionable behavior.

Sigmund Freud had much to say about awareness. The weird surmises of Freud, though long since disproved, are accepted by many even at this late date. He championed the idea that within us is the Id, consisting of basic drives that clamor for fulfilment. On the outside, he said, are forces, the Super-Ego, that tend to restrict the body from complete gratification. As a result of conflict between Id and Super-Ego, the individual settles for a compromise. This clash results in the

Ego, the real self. Freud was persuaded that restriction of the Id by the Super-Ego is the chief cause of mental illness. He felt that doing what comes naturally makes for mental health and physical well-being.

The awareness cult has little time for awareness of God. The apostle Paul warned those who refused to have God in their knowledge that they would be given up to reprobate minds (Rom. 1:28). He also warned that those who are interested only in self-approval, apart from approval of God, are without understanding (2 Cor. 10:12).

Self-awareness is good, provided it is accompanied by an even greater awareness of the power and majesty of God, together with strict adherence to His commands. "Jehovah knoweth the way of the righteous; but the way of the wicked shall perish" (Psalm 1:6).

31

Demons

From ghoulies and ghosties and long-leggety beasties
And things that go bump in the night,
Good Lord, deliver us!

A world-wide wave of occultism and Satanism has been aided and abetted by a number of foul motion pictures dealing with demons. According to reviews the movies are blatantly pornographic, scatological, and exceedingly repulsive. In this connection a nationally syndicated writer tells of clergymen who, supposedly, have performed feats of exorcism.

Obviously, demonic possession occurred in Old Testament times. It is equally obvious that such possession was commonplace during Jesus' earthly ministry as well as later during the apostolic period. You recall, of course, Paul's exorcising of the maid with "a spirit of divination" recorded in Acts 16.

Those possessed of demons lived during a period that also witnessed the direct operation of the Holy Spirit, a phenomenon that ceased upon completion of the perfect law of liberty (James 1:25) in keeping with Paul's statement about the demise of special spiritual gifts (1 Cor. 13:10).

So what is our premise? Simply this: During that period when unclean spirits were allowed to enter the physical bodies of men and women, the evil spirits were often exorcised by the much more powerful Holy Spirit. (See Matt. 4:24; 8:16; 9:32; 12:24, 26, 43; Mark 1:24, 32, 34; 3:11-12; Luke 4:41; 6:18; 10:17; 13:32.) However, now that the Holy Spirit operates through the word it seems readily apparent that demons are no longer permitted to posses a human body. This would be too great an advantage on the side of evil.

Faith in God gave protection in the long ago and faith in our time will enable the saints to quench "all the fiery darts of the evil one" (Eph. 6:16).

32

Costly Experiment

A story in a national magazine featured Will and Ariel Durant. The Durants now deceased, were co-authors of the famous *Story of Civilization* series. The 11th and final volume of the series is entitled *The Age of Napoleon*.

There was a time when Dr. Durant was full of quips and snide remarks about religion in general and Christianity in particular. By his own admission he became rather mellow. In his nineties, shortly before his death, he looked with some dismay upon the world he had studied and written about for so many years. From a lofty intellectual perch he concluded, "Today we live in an age of chaos. In morality, art, and music, we're floundering around. I used to say art was the transformation of chaos into order. Now it seems to be the transformation of order into chaos."

Perhaps the most significant statement resulting from the interview came when the noted author said, "The great experiment we're engaged in is whether a moral code can survive without the support of supernatural beliefs. That's the crux of the matter." Crux it is! Long ago Dr. Durant was a pusher of the experiment. In his early years he bolted religion in favor of the heady thinking of young radicals.

It would have been well drawing on his enormous knowledge of history, if he had accepted a truth that has been demonstrated again and again in every age. That truth is this: No individual or group or nation, having thrown religion to the winds, has been able to survive. It is a truth that is clearly and succinctly stated in the 23rd verse of the 10th chapter of Jeremiah: "O Jehovah, I know that the way of man is not in himself; it is not in man that walketh to direct his steps."

33

Caveat Emptor

"I'll buy that!" So say those wishing to express approval of a statement, or situation, or life style.

Before me is a book purporting to present new concepts of freedom. It has been high on the nation's bestseller lists. Reviews are ecstatic, as indicated by these samples: "Crackles with electrifying insights and understanding of our deepest predicament." "Has shown me how to be free." "Should be on the bedside stand of any who feel trapped."

Obviously, the reviewers have bought the theories. "Right," the author says, "is *anything* that will bring you happiness. Wrong is *anything* that will cause you unhappiness." He goes on to say that talents are to be fully utilized in bestowing happiness upon the "one person you understand well enough to do it efficiently—yourself."

It would be difficult to contemplate a philosophy more abhorrent to our Lord and more fully guaranteed to end in moral and spiritual disaster. Such an outlook is the antithesis of Christ's exhortation to deny self, take up the cross daily, and follow him (Luke 9:23).

Freedom from restraint, so popular these days—even among those in high places—is not to be equated with genuine freedom. Unrestrained pleasure seekers are said to be dead while they live (1 Tim. 5:6). In the end they must bow to that monster called disillusionment. On the other hand, the world and its ills are conquered by those who heed the inspired plea of the apostle Paul: "I beseech you therefore, brethren, by the mercies of God, to present your bodies a living sacrifice, holy, acceptable to God, which is your spiritual service" (Rom. 12:1).

Caveat emptor, let the buyer beware.

34

Cops and Robbers

In time past a favorite game of youngsters growing up in the city was cops and robbers. Whereas even then there was a decided preference to play the part of the robbers, it was understood that eventually the thugs would be caught and deposited in the slammer. In those dear dead days almost beyond recall there was an ingrained respect for the law and for those who enforced the law. No matter how titillating to pretend being on the wrong side of the law, it was accepted by the children that crime does not pay. This attitude stemmed from their firm belief that right is right, wrong is wrong and, inevitably, reward and/or punishment could be expected.

Somewhere along the line, however, a not-so-subtle change began to take place. Right was still right if one wanted it that way but on the other hand wrong was equally acceptable. Thus an Ambassador to the United Nations excused looting on the fallacious grounds that looters were hungry—which, presumably, is why they showed a preference for color television sets.

The same degree of laissez-faire is seen in attitudes toward the entire gamut of unlawful and sinful practices. And comes now an amazing admission by an erstwhile guardian of the law. Lewis R. Sutin, judge of the New Mexico Court of Appeals, sees nothing wrong in the behavior of a woman who seduced a 15-year old boy. As to the woman's having caused or encouraged the boy's delinquency the judge opined, "As a matter of law, I say that (she) did not." Presumably the judge looks askance at the biblical account of Joseph's virtuous refusal, in a similar circumstance, to yield to the wiles of Potiphar's wife (Gen. 39:7-20). He concluded with the statement, "The legislature (of N. M.) abolished fornication as a crime. In doing so, it cast aside the ancient religious doctrine that forbids such practices . . . the conduct did not violate the mores of the 20th century."

How can one respect a law that violates the law of God? Peter and the other apostles provide an answer: "We must obey God rather than men" (Acts 5:29). The judge's statement is but another indication of our nation's crumbling morality. Those who persist in following so ungodly a course "shall not inherit the kingdom of heaven" (Gal. 5:19-21).

Who are the cops and who are the robbers?

35

Blanket Indictments

A bank teller doctors his records and goes on a spectacular spending spree. When the embezzlement is brought to light by examiners the man becomes a guest of the state.

Upon spotting the item in the newspaper a reader grumps, "They're all alike; if they think they have a chance they'll steal."

A police officer learns that a grocery store is a gambling front. When offered hush money he accepts. Superiors learn of the officer's perfidy. He is dismissed and later joins the bank teller in the pokey. The unsavory news prompts a man to comment, "Yeah, they'll do it every time; the police are bigger offenders than anybody."

A preacher runs off with another man's wife. The news is bruited about. A man who never goes to church says smugly, "That's why I don't go for this church bit; all the people who go are rank hypocrites."

It is amazing that anyone could be taken in by such absurdities. Though some bank employees have been known to steal, a bank could not stay in business if none could be trusted. Though some policemen have been guilty of crime, they are the exceptions. And when a preacher is guilty of a lustful sin the news is widely heralded because such behavior is completely out of character with a servant of the Lord.

Even Elijah was once touched by the no-faith-in-anybody virus. He complained, ". . . The children of Israel have forsaken thy covernant, thrown down thine altars, and slain thy prophets with the sword; and I, even I only, am left . . ." (1 Kings 19:14).

Elijah's blanket indictment was in error. Seven thousand refused to bow to Baal. As in Elijah's day, so in ours. Exceptions to virtuous behavior receive reams of publicity, but exceptions do not establish the norm.

36

The Existential Outlook

Absolute principles of truth, such as those stated in the Ten Commandments and the Sermon on the Mount, are denied by those whose vision is distorted by humanistic philosophies. Humanism, another name for atheism, holds that there are no supernatural forces above nature. Obviously, this conception rules out the very existence of God as well as the divinity of Christ and the inspiration of the scriptures. Man, they tell us, is on his own, sailing a stormy sea without compass, rudder, or destination. Small wonder that the sharers of this dismal view often try to find satisfying experiences in drugs, illicit liaisons and, in some instances, by rebellion against authority.

Existentialists insist there is no possibility of achieving a rational and valid conclusion; instead, they advocate a leap in the dark, hoping to find rewarding encounters along the way. Their outlook places them on a collision course with utter hopelessness. Jean-Paul Sartre and Albert Camus tell us that we live in an absurd universe. According to their teaching, man's quest for truth is akin to a search for the end of the rainbow. Consequently, it is absurd to think in terms of absolutes in ethics and morals for there is no such thing as absolute right and absolute wrong.

Apart from the foregoing inanities, we know that in the physical realm, whether in China or Africa or here at home, water comes from the combination of two parts hydrogen and one part oxygen, without fail. And in the moral realm, just as surely, righteousness exalts a nation while sin is always a reproach to any people (Prov. 14:34). There will never be a time when it is right and proper to kill, steal, commit adultery, bear false witness, or take the name of the Lord in vain.

There is a need for existentialists and situation ethicists to answer a question raised by our Lord: "If I say truth, why do you not believe me?" (John 8:46).

37

On Reaching Sixty-Five

In the manner of Samuel Pepys: Up betimes on my natal day with grateful thoughts anent the attaining of three score and five years, but not without wonder at the brevity of life.

A recent unsigned essay states in part, "A person of 65 cannot be expected to carry the physical load he toted with ease when he was 35. He can, however, seek opportunity with the ardor of youth." Whereas young people are often pursued by opportunity, it is a fact of life that with the passage of years the pursued, of necessity, become the pursuers.

Brutus, in *Julius Caesar,* says to his fellow conspirator Cassius, "There is a tide in the affairs of men which, taken at the flood, leads on to fortune; omitted, all the voyage of their life is bound in shallows and in miseries." As a former dweller on an arm of the mighty atlantic, this scrivener long has been fascinated by the power and precision of tides. Tides of the sea are predictable and constant. This is not the case with the tides of life. Thus when one reaches 65 he sometimes looks back in wonder, often with inexpressible regret, and never with complete satisfaction, over the manner in which opportunities have been handled.

At 65 one must decide, having received his portion of joy and sorrow, whether to drift into cynicism and discontent or follow a course of happiness and good cheer. The latter, it would seem, can be maintained by rejoicing in God's grace and in the wonders of His creation, in the companionship of dear friends and loved ones, in the majesty of great music and literature, in the knowledge that one's work meets a need and, above all else, in the abiding hope that one's "labor is not in vain in the Lord" (1 Cor. 15:58).

'Twas a long day of visitation with children and grandchildren, of eating well if not wisely, of much good talk and observance of pleasing antics of little ones in whom we are perhaps inordinately proud. And so to bed.

38
Anxiety

Anguish deals with that which is known. Anxiety, on the other hand, has to do with the unknown. There is entirely too much anguish in a world torn by heartache and suffering. There is even more anxiety. Fear of the unknown is ever with us.

Every day is scare day for millions. The average person is faced with narrow brushes with death in traffic, with the prospect of losing a job, with being wiped out by hospital expenses, with spiraling inflation that mocks at frugality, with misunderstandings in office, factory and home, and, of course, with fearsome headlines and newscasts relating to crime, crises, and corruption. Some are persuaded the tranquilizer should replace the eagle as our national emblem.

Anxiety is as old as mankind. Library shelves are overflowing with books on the subject. Various approaches are being utilized in the hope that peace of mind may be achieved. Unfortunately, the Bible, the greatest of all books on the subject, is widely ignored.

In his book, *Crisis In Psychiatry and Religion,* Hobart Mowrer says, "Religion, to which we have traditionally looked for redemption from evil and guidance in the good life has all but abandoned its claim to competence in these matters." We feel Mowrer's accusation is too severe. There are still many who are intent on finding the peace promised by our Lord even as they accept without rancor the trials from which none may expect immunity.

Midway in his great Sermon on the Mount our Savior offers a solution to anxiety. "Be not anxious for your life, what ye shall eat, or what ye shall drink; nor yet for your body, what ye shall put on. Is not the life more than the food, and the body than the raiment?" Following his analogy dealing with birds, flowers, and physical limitations of the body, Jesus reminds

45

his hearers that the heavenly Father knows their needs. Then comes that great charge and promise: "Seek ye first his kingdom, and his righteousness; and all these things shall be added unto you" (Matt. 6:25, 33).

39
Purely Personal

This scriven deals neither with earth-shaking matters of state nor obscure biblical technicalities, but rather with changes in attitude which have affected manners and modes of dress. The subject comes under the heading of opinion and, obviously, where opinion is concerned one is free to accept or reject.

When girls and women began dressing casually to the point of slovenliness, many felt it was a fad that shortly would pass away. They were wrong. The unkempt look continues. It may be seen, and shuddered at, almost everywhere.

Remember when men wore hats and doffed them in the presence of women? and rushed to open doors for members of the fair sex? and never, never brushed by in front of a woman? Those days are long gone. In fairness to these churlish males, let it be said that a woman in tank top and jeans, or halter and shorts, offers little incentive for chivalry. (Aw c'mon, you do remember that word.) Conversely, an equal number of men seem to covet the slouchy, disheveled look.

Time was when lady-like bearing was balanced by gentlemanly behavior, in dress, grooming, and manners. For example, in his essay on "Poor Relations" Charles Lamb wrote, "No woman dresses below herself from caprice." But that was 150 years ago. Now women, as well as their male counterparts, avidly and intentionally dress below themselves, cherishing an appearance that at times borders on the absurd.

We have become somewhat weary of this constant plethora of dishabille and we long to see men and women in street and marketplace who are not only neat in appearance but, as to gender, are immediately recognizable.

40

Hiccups and Preaching

An old story, now making the rounds again, has to do with a man who asked a doctor friend what to do for hiccups. The doctor, without a word, struck his friend a solid blow on the chin, knocking him to the floor. The man got up and shakily demanded a reason for such treatment. "Why, to cure you of course," the doctor replied, "you don't have hiccups now do you?" "No," said the now irate and erstwhile friend, "and what's more I never did have 'em—but my wife does and she's out in the car."

Time was when preachers delivered hammer blows designed to shock men and women into a realization of the necessity of obedience to the primary commands of the gospel. As time went on, however, their blows often rained down on those who had long since obeyed those very commands. Having heard, they had believed, repented, confessed Christ as the Son of God, and had been baptized in His name. Yet these Christians heard over and over such familiar lessons as, "What Must I Do To Be Saved?" "The Philippian Jailor," "Why Tarriest Thou?" etc.

Now the pendulum has swung to the opposite extreme. Preachers are extolling the merits as well as the necessity of Christian living as, of course, they should. But oftentimes in their audiences are many who have never obeyed the gospel. It is not a matter, as with certain internationally known evangelists, of deliberately withholding information relating to the first principles of the gospel. Instead, theirs is the mistaken idea that this information is too well known to bear repeating. The truth of the matter is that it needs repeating. We need to preach on Christian living for that is a subject that fills the greater portion of the New Testament. At the same time, we must never for a moment forget the alien's urgent need to hear of those things required of him that he might be added to the Lord's church.

41

Ipse Dixit

Every now and then the expression "ipse dixit" finds its way into the comments of politicians (who perhaps are rather good at it), as well as the writings of teachers, reformers, preachers and others. Readers who are unable to come up with a clear definition, in spite of the context in which the words occur, may ignore them and trust the meaning, somehow, will materialize at a later time. The alternative involves the onerous chore of turning to the dictionary. Random House Dictionary defines ipse dixit (which sounds like an apt name for a rock group) as "an assertion without proof, or he himself said it."

In the wide spectrum of religion we encounter numerous examples of ipse dixiting all over the place. For example, there is the learned theologian who avers (a theologian never *says*; he always *avers*), "Baptism is a part of apostolic symbolism that obviously is no longer essential among believers." Then there is the fellow who seldom if ever reads the Bible but stoutly maintains, "I feel that I am a Christian although I have never thought it necessary to make a formal acknowledgement or confession. Also, I have never felt it worthwhile to submit to any set of requirements. Nor do I think it necessary to attend the formal worship of the church." Oh ipse, watch your dixit!

Closer home is that disciple who boasts, "I never attend the evening worship or the mid-week Bible study because you can't show me a place where the Bible says it's necessary." The man is right, yet oh so wrong. In addition, he can't be shown a place in the Bible where it says he must meet with the saints on Sunday morning at exactly 9, 10, or 11 o'clock. But it does say, "not forsaking our own assembling together, as the custom of some is, but exhorting one another; and so much the more, as ye see the day drawing nigh" (Heb. 10:25). And we also read, "upon the first day of the week, when we were gathered together to break bread . . ." (Acts 20:27). Then, of course, there are such passages as these: "Give diligence to present thyself approved . . ." (2 Tim. 2:15). "Be not fashioned according to this world: but . . . transformed by the renewing of your mind" (Rom. 12:2), and "grow in the grace and knowledge of our Lord and Savior Jesus Christ" (2 Pet. 3:18), all of which are extremely difficult if not impossible when we fail to avail ourselves of worship and learning opportunities during our brief earthly sojourn. Up, up, ipse dixit—and away!

42
Fear

Fear has been defined as "painful emotion marked by alarm; disquiet, anxiety, uncertainty, lack of self-assurance." Some portion of the definition describes every human being at some station of his journey through life. Significantly, the things we fear are accurate indices to the lives we live.

Fear has two faces. Whereas it can destroy, fear is also capable of acting as a buffer to keep us from harm. Much of the Bible is devoted to alleviating fear. Yet a certain kind of fear is shown to be essential to one's well-being. In a world torn by countless fears and phobias, men need to weigh their fears on the divine scales of truth.

Some of the things that fill our hearts with fear are real. Some are not. However, the end result is the same. Groundless fears can be as harmful to the nervous system as those that are genuine. Though "fears may be liars" the victim seldom detects the falsehood. Shaving cream placed on the mouth of a gentle dog by pranksters will give the animal the appearance of a dreaded rabies infection. The danger is imaginary, the resulting fear is no less than if the dog were mad.

Some things need to be feared. A careening automobile, an avalanche, a crumbling building, a flash flood, a false doctrine—these are to be feared. But deadly, useless fears must be overcome in order to achieve a degree of peace and equanimity. Paul puts it this way, "If God is for us, who is against us?" (Rom. 8:31).

We are aware that a jungle taboo is utterly ridiculous, but what about fear of a black cat? The diviner of a central African tribe may have much in common with the highly articulate dabbler in glossolalia. A civilized man may have qualms about spilled salt or Friday the 13th while the savage cringes before a pin-laden doll. In either case, baseless fear is an enemy that must be overcome.

There is but one way to overcome fear in this world and that is to center our fear (reverence) upon God. "The fear of Jehovah is the beginning of wisdom; and the knowledge of the Holy One is understanding" (Prov. 9:10). "Fear God, and keep his commandments; for this is the whole duty of man" (Eccles. 12:13). Freedom from fear is a great part of the mission of faith. ". . . Let not your heart be troubled, neither let it be fearful" (John 14:27).

43

My Corny Friends

The word *corny*, meaning gauche, has been used indiscriminately to describe the ordinary citizenry of our land, especially the law-abiding, the payers of honest debts, and those whose speech is not larded with obscenities. The word has also been used to describe God-fearing, Bible-believing, obedient servants of our Lord. Obviously, corny is a word that takes in considerable territory.

I have friends who read their Bibles daily, attend worship Sunday morning and evening, enjoy the mid-week service, attend gospel meetings, give generously of their means, visit the sick, provide food for the hungry, and are found "instant in season and out of season." How corny can they get?

My corny friends are not unaware of Hemingway, Faulkner, and Michener. However, they are more at home with Dickens, Twain, and Melville. Among the poets they prefer Tennyson to Baudelaire. As for writers on religious themes, they agree that C. S. Lewis wins hands down over the likes of Joseph Fletcher. And they have a special affection for Campbell, Scott, Lipscomb, Harding, Sewell, et al.

Whereas these cornball friends are not averse to a funny story, they are turned off by that which is deliberately salacious. They take seriously the exhortation of the apostle Paul who said, "Walk in wisdom toward them that are without, redeeming the time. Let your speech be always with grace, seasoned with salt, that ye may know how ye ought to answer each one" (Col. 4:5-6). They share the belief that the pure in heart shall see God (Matt. 5:8), and they are not unmindful of the Master's admonition, " . . . Ye shall know the truth, and the truth shall make you free" (John 8:32).

Yep, I'm thankful for my friends, the cornier the better.

44

Man's Worst Enemy

"Man in this moment of history has emerged in greater supremacy over the forces of nature than has ever been dreamed of before. There lies before him, if he wishes, a golden age of peace and progress. All is in his hand. He has only to conquer his last and worst enemy—himself." So said Winston Churchill. The time was March 28, 1950. The place was the House of Commons.

With the swift passage of years since "the man of the century" uttered his stirring pronouncement, vast changes have taken place. We have witnessed advances over the forces of nature perhaps even beyond the fertile imagination of Sir Winston.

In our computerized age, with its far-ranging wizardry in electronic technology, that which was once deemed impossible has become commonplace. Space probes spanning millions of miles are supplying information heretofore unknowable. The electron microscope, meantime, has revealed astounding secrets of the infinitesimal world of the atom. Problems that once taxed the ingenuity of mathematicians are now resolved with the press of a button. Information vital to travel, banking, logistics, medicine, and the innumerable needs of business and industry, is produced in seconds.

But with all these marvels the last and worst enemy, alluded to by Churchill, has not been conquered. Man's stubborn will resists the overtures of a loving heavenly Father. For example, out of the probe of the planet Venus, a spectacular feat involving computations that stagger the imagination, has come a news story stating the new findings "could cause scientists to change their theories on the origin of the solar system." It is as though these gifted men are completely unaware that "in the beginning God created the heavens and the earth" and that the stupendous vault of heaven, with all its stars and planets, came about because God willed it, and all these marvels are but the work of His fingers (Gen. 1:1; Psalm 8:3).

"The heavens declare the glory of God; and the firmament showeth his handiwork. . . . Let everything that hath breath praise Jehovah" (Psalm 19:1; 150:6).

45
Fortitude

We all have handicaps of one kind or another. There are no exceptions. People are overweight and underweight, hard of hearing and arthritic; some are concerned about their children and others are concerned about parents, or husbands or wives; some are in financial straits and others are lonely or hounded by vain regrets. Those so minded easily find reason for giving up, although there are far more reasons for continuing on. No one individual has a corner on health and well-being; no one bears burdens never before borne by others. Whereas the prophet speaks of "labor and sorrow" (Psalm 90:10) accruing to those who reach fourscore years, he does not limit such to the aged.

There is a story in Paul McElroy's *Wings of Recovery* of an attractive girl who stopped beside the bed of a stone-deaf war victim. As the deaf soldier talked, the girl scribbled answers on a pad. The young man was terribly discouraged. "Please come to see me again," he begged, "it's awful not knowing what people around you are saying." The girl wrote. "I don't know that it's so awful. I'm as deaf as you. You must learn to read lips as I have been reading yours."

It was my privilege, in historic Westminster Castle, a magnificent building dating back to 1097 A.D., to stand beside a plaque marking the spot where Sir Winston Churchill's body lay in state. His brave words delivered to the students of Harrow came to mind: "Never give in! Never give in! Never, Never, Never, Never—in nothing great or small, large or petty—Never give in except to convictions of honor and good sense."

Churchill's words will be long remembered, but words greater than Churchill's, that will endure as long as the world stands, have come from the pen of the apostle Paul. More than 1900 years ago he wrote, "We are pressed on every side, yet not

53

straitened; perplexed, yet not unto dispair; pursued, yet not forsaken; smitten down, yet not destroyed. Wherefore we faint not; but though our outward man is decaying, yet our inward man is renewed day by day. For our light affliction, which is for the moment, worketh for us more and more exceedingly an eternal weight of glory" (2 Cor. 4:8-9, 16-17). And you are aware of course that this same great apostle said, "I press on toward the goal unto the prize of the high calling of God in Christ Jesus" (Phil. 3:14).

46
God and Caesar

An editoral in the *Wall Street Journal* points out that at the time Saul of Tarsus was journeying to Damascus the entire world was in bondage. Rome, in those far off days, let it be known that Tiberius Caesar was master of all. While there was stability in society and government, there was oppression for those who dared take exception to the brand of justice meted out by Rome. Consequently, the executioners were kept busy.

Those who opposed Jesus tried to ensnare him. What better way than to have him say something publicly that could be interpreted as contrary to the vaunted Roman Law? It was to be expected, therefore, that eventually the enemy would get around to asking, "What thinkest thou? Is it lawful to give tribute unto Caesar, or not?" The record states that Jesus perceived their wicked scheme and asked. "Why make ye trial of me, ye hypocrites?" Then he asked to be shown the tribute money. "Whose is this image and superscription?" he asked. They replied, "Caesar's." Our Lord then said, "Render therefore unto Caesar the things that are Caesar's; and unto God the things that are God's."

With the passing of nearly twenty centuries, the words of
our Lord are still applicable. There is an urgent need to understand what is Caesar's and what is God's—and to act accor-
dingly. Whereas we are commanded to pray for and be subject
to the powers that be (1 Tim. 2:1-2; Rom. 13:1-7), we are also
taught by approved example to obey God when a choice must
be made between good and evil (Acts 5:29).

Christians make good citizens. They obey the laws of the
land. They do not cheat or steal or engage in vandalism.
Neither do they give themselves over to sensuality and riot.
They live by God's rule—which calls for rendering "unto
Caesar the things that are Caesar's; and unto God the things
that are God's."

The nations that fail to differentiate between God and
Caesar soon find themselves under the heel of Caesar. "Blessed is the nation whose God is Jehovah" (Psalm 33:12).

47

Eis
(Getting Back to Basics)

We were interested in a reply received by a friend to his
letter protesting statement of a speaker on national radio who
said baptism is in no way essential to salvation.

A member of the radio speaker's team wrote, "We are not
in agreement with the doctrine which teaches that baptism is
necessary for salvation." From a booklet accompanying the
letter we gleaned the following: " . . . All who are in the
mainstream of evangelical Christianity agree that water baptism is not essential to salvation. . . . Since the Bible explicity
teaches that salvation is received by faith, and since the
preposition *eis* often has the meaning *because of* or *in rela-
tion to*, Mark 1:4 must be seen as a declaration that John

baptized because of the forgiveness of sins. The same holds true of Peter's statement in Acts 2:38, where he pleads with his audience to repent, and to be baptized as a testimonial of the forgiveness of their sins."

We are reminded of G. C. Brewer's statement that a great many religious writers "are skating about on thin *eis.*"

In passing it should be noted that baptism is part of our Lord's Great Commission (Matt. 28:19-20); it is commanded and must be obeyed (Mark 16:15-16; 2 Thess. 1:7-8); it was among those things Paul was told he "must" do (Acts 9:6); it is for the forgiveness of sins (Acts 2:38) and the means of getting into Christ (Gal. 3:27; Rom. 6:3) where one becomes a new creature (2 Cor. 5:17) with the washing away of sins (Acts 22:16; 1 Pet. 3:21).

In his *Commentary on Acts,* H. Leo Boles lists authorities, including Thayer, Schaff, Strong, Willmarth and others, who translate *eis* "in order to," "into," "to," "toward," "unto," and "to the end."

W. D. Frazee's *Reminiscences and Sermons* was published by the Gospel Advocate nearly a hundred years ago. In it Frazee records S. K. Houshour's reply to those who insisted that *into* was a bad translation. Houshour, a noted linguist, discounted his ability, stating he was familiar with only six languages. The point had been made that "Moses went up into the mountain" and therefore the proper inference to be drawn was that going down into the water should read, *going down to,* or *nearby* the water. Houshour's reply resulted in his becoming known affectionately thereafter as the puzzled Dutchman. It is, in part as follows: "I ish so glad I vas here for I has had exblained vhat I never pelieved before. We read dat Taniel vas cast into te ten of lions, and came out alive. . . . Now it ish exblained. He vas shust close py. De Hebrew children vas cast into de firish furnace . . . but . . . dey vas shust cast py or close to de firish furnace. It is said dat Jonah vas taken into de whalesh pelly. Now I never could pelieve dat, but it is all plain, he shust shumpt on to his pack and rode ashore. And now, Mr. Breacher, if you vill shust exblain two more passages. One of dem ish vhere it saish de vicked shall pe cast into a lake dat burns mit fire. Shall I pe cast into dat lake if I am vicked, or shust close py or near to, shust near enough to pe comfortable? De odder passage is dat vich saish blessed are dey who do dese commandments, dat dey may enter in troo de gates into de city. Now, if I vas good, shall I go into de city or only shust close py or near enough to see vhat I have lost?"

48

On the Elusiveness of Sleep

Some time ago a letter came from a dear friend, a former co-worker, who is slowly recuperating from a long and trying illness. His letter begins, "It is two in the morning and hardly a time for playing kitten on the keys on the old Royal, but I took some pain medication earlier in the evening that sometimes induces drowsiness; this time I am as wide awake as a barn owl. I think God in his goodness gives us sleep to comfort sorrow, and yesterday brought it in a heavy dose. Now I need someone to talk to when, as Scott Fitzgerald wrote, 'In the dark night of the soul it is always three o'clock in the morning.' "

The letter was read just prior to the reading of a book that meticulously outlined the horrors that will be visited upon this planet should full-scale nuclear warfare dissolve major cities, leaving utter desolation for its few survivors amid radio-active lands and seas. When at last the book was put aside, in the early morning, sleep had been routed by dire, racing thoughts.

The letter, as well as the book, brought to my wide-eyed state the yearning voiced by Macbeth for "sleep that knits up the ravell'd sleeve of care." Sleeplessness, of course, is experienced by both the evil and the just. And far better at such times than Shakespeare's measured lines are the reassuring words of courage and comfort found in God's holy book.

"When thou liest down, thou shalt not be afraid: Yea, thou shalt lie down, and thy sleep shall be sweet. Be not afraid of sudden fear, Neither of the desolation of the wicked, when it cometh: For Jehovah will be thy confidence, And will keep thy foot from being taken" (Prov. 3:24-26).

49

Distinctiveness

A leader among the Quakers once said it was a sad day when his religious group became respectable. He was toying with the word respectable, of course, because that which prompted his remark was the fact that his people were no longer distinctive but had become very much like the denominations around them. Perhaps such outstanding Quakers as James Michener and Richard M. Nixon whose writings (expletives deleted) are so well-known, could comment further on their erstwhile leader's observation.

But suppose we look at ourselves. Time was when our preaching, teaching, and Christian living were indeed distinctive. We were regarded as "the people who are different." When reading or hearing a sermon it was readily apparent whether or not the speaker or writer was one of ours. As for drinking, dancing, engaging in doubtful recreation, or indulging in the venal and salacious—such things were taboo. This stance came about not because of custom but because of our respect for the word of God.

Now our preachers have more education and fewer rough edges. Their language is smooth and, too often, so are they. Can it be that preachers, like many politicians, are listening to the people rather than having the people listen to them—as they present the unsearchable riches of God?

"For it is a rebellious people, lying children, children that will not hear the law of Jehovah; that say to the seers, See not; and to the prophets, Prophesy not unto us right things, speak unto us smooth things, prophesy deceits, get you out of the way, turn aside out of the path, cause the Holy One of Israel to cease from before us" (Isa. 30:9-11). Then there is the more familiar but equally unheeded passage: "Preach the word; be urgent in season, out of season; reprove, rebuke, exhort, with all longsuffering and teaching. For the time will come when they will not endure the sound doctrine; but, having itching ears, will heap to themselves teachers after their own lusts; and will turn away their ears from the truth, and turn aside unto fables" (2 Tim. 4:2-4).

Paul warned, "the time will come." It should be obvious that the time has come.

50

Curmudgeonly Thoughts on the Demise of Generic Usage

Time was when the word "man," along with the pronoun "he," was used in its generic sense and was readily understood to mean both men and women. Today, what with the aroused ire of ERA, generic terminology is going the way of the dodo. Also, time was when the familiar phrase, "battle of the sexes," was thought to be a matter (more or less) of friendly give and take on intellectual and emotional levels where sparring was regarded as normal and par for the course. Today the battle continues but with a difference. In place, for example, of men's humorous (?) remarks about women's hats (objects seldom seen these days) there is greater likelihood that comments will be directed toward women's competitiveness. Conversely, whereas women once complained mildly of men's stubbornness (can it be possible?), the fray has shifted to such things as equality and discrimination.

If there breathes a poor, misguided male who doesn't believe these obvious truths, let him try writing a sentence such as "Everyone is free to serve in his chosen field." Unless the wording is changed to an awkward "his or her chosen field" or, worse still, to "one's chosen field," there are sure to be repercussions. Who would deny that the ladies are free to speak their mind, to say nothing of commenting testily on the male chauvinism demonstrated by a careless writer who dares use the generic "his." Such attitudes abound even when the complainant is blissfully unaware of the derivation of "chauvinism."

These thoughts, fraught with danger, came to mind while reading the morning paper in which a picture story of a nun in Washington appeared during the Pope's highly publicized visit. She was shown pleading (castigating?) him for his stand, a remarkably biblical stand in most respects, on a woman's place in the church. Despite the emotional plea of the nun it seems the Pope would have none of it. Pun my word, that ain't bad.

The denominational world has been shaken by rebellion against a statement by Paul (not John Paul) and, alas, the church of our Lord has not escaped unscathed. "I permit not a woman to teach," he said, "nor to have dominion over a man, but to be in quietness" (1 Tim. 2:12). In this passage the words "man" and "woman" are used in a specific sense and are easily understood. It is understood further that "quietness" does not mean absolute silence in the assembly; otherwise, women would be forbidden to sing. In the setting, the assembly, women are not allowed to teach, thus taking an authoritative stance over men. We didn't write the Bible; that's the way it is.

While we're on the subject, what did Jesus mean when he said, "What is a *man* profited, if he shall gain the whole world, and lose his own soul?" Are women excluded?

60

51

Home

It's a fact: The sweet influence of the home is on the wane. The constant derisive and devisive teaching of many who are in roles of authority has had a disastrous effect on the thinking of modern man. He has, in large part, accepted the supposed freedoms offered by a philosophy aimed at alienation and disruption of all family responsibility.

Before we yield to despair, however, let it be said that the home is still a going concern. It is the oldest institution on earth, a bulwark in a crumbling world. The enemy, through the years and especially in recent times, has loosed great salvos against the home. Some in high places insist that the home is a back number, an anachronism, that it has filled a place in primitive culture, but now it is no longer needed.

Even so, HOME is a word dear to the hearts of godly men and women everywhere. It has thrilled poets and fascinated soldiers, prisoners, and world travelers. It has warmed the prodigal and encouraged the obedient. Home is a word that has brought assurance to the young and comfort to the aged. Home is the place where joys and sorrows are shared as well as the highest of hopes and aspirations.

Pliny, Roman statesman and scholar, a contemporary of our Lord's apostles, coined the phrase "Home is where the heart is." As the home goes, so goes the nation—and the world. The home is God's device for the preservation of mankind. The Christian home is a place of warmth and enduring love. In it are ties of affection undimmed by time and space. It is a composite of faith and discipline and is tempered with loyalty; respect, and loving devotion.

Thanks be to God for Christian homes.

52

Peace

Sir Walter Raleigh, English courtier, navigator, historian and poet, lived a life of adventure. He engaged in piracy against the Spaniards, explored the North American coast from Florida to North Carolina, fell in and out of favor with royalty and, after Queen Elizabeth's death, was executed on charges of conspiracy.

On the scaffold Raleigh made a brief defense of his actions, concluding with the statement, "I entreat you all to join with me in prayer, being a man full of all vanity and having lived a sinful life in all sinful callings, that the great God of heaven would forgive me, cast away my sins from me, and receive me into everlasting life. So I take my leave of you all, making my peace with God." When Raleigh's head was placed on the block a witness said it should be turned toward the east. The condemned man responded, "What matter how the head lies, if the heart be right?" These were his last words.

As our Lord neared the end of his earthly ministry he said, " . . . In me ye may have peace. In the world ye have tribulation: but be of good cheer; I have overcome the world" (John 16:33). Later, Paul spoke of "the peace of God, which passeth all understanding" which, he said, "shall guard your hearts and your thoughts in Christ Jesus" (Phil. 4:7).

Raleigh, even as others in his situation, longed for peace with God. His last words indicate a sense of peace as he bravely faced death. But was his hope "built on nothing less than Jesus' blood and righteousness?" And down through the centuries, what of those who have waited, as did Raleigh, till the very last moment to make their peace with God? They, as we, are in the hands of that One who shall judge the world in righteousness (Acts 17:31) who said, "He that believeth and is baptized shall be saved; but he that disbelieveth shall be condemned." (Mark 16:16) and who asked, "Why call ye me, Lord, Lord, and do not the things which I say?" (Luke 6:46).

53
Giveaways

Liberals in government are more than eagar to give away tax moneys that otherwise might be applied toward the reduction of our enormous national debt. Giveaways have reached the point where a large percentage of the nation's working force is employed by government for the express purpose of furthering its burgeoning giveaways. But beyond giveaways to professional indigents at home and abroad (as well as to those who are genuinely in need), liberals are pressing to give away our lands, our defenses and the very freedoms established by our forefathers. Some time ago Aleksandr Solzhenitsyn stated that it is the importation of American technology that is saving the Soviets. Thus it is especially frightening that the Soviets are said to consider nuclear warfare to be inevitable. Leonid Brezhnev insists there is no room for neutrality and compromise in the struggle between American and Soviet ideologies. So much for detente.

Since this is not a political treatise we shall not pursue the matter further, other than to make an obvious application. The church of our Lord is also faced with liberalism, and liberals in the church are also dead set on giveaways. They are contemptuous of those who would walk in the old paths; they are critical of efforts to "contend earnestly for the faith;" and they would readily open the doors to those who discount the necessity of following the New Testament as the only guide for faith and practice. That inroads have been made by these forces is readily apparent when one considers the defections of those who substitute subjective and experiential religion for revealed truth. Invariably, such practices culminate in the supposed baptism of the Holy Spirit with a concomitant wooing of charismata and glossolalia, thus harking back to the Montanists of the second century.

It was a sad day for the church when certain of its liberal members decided that Pentecostalism, with its unscriptural, heathenish gibberish, is worthy of emulation. This is a give-away that must not be tolerated by believers.

54

Floating Down the Etymological Stream

A review sent this scribe scurrying in search of William Espy's opus, *O Thou Improper, Thou Uncommon Noun.* This sprightly tome assures me that those who resort to boycott are engaging in a course of action named for Captain Charles Cunningham Boycott, whose servants left him and to whom grocers refused to sell food. As for lynch, it seems that Charles Lynch, a Virginia planter, employed extra-legal methods in punishing Tories during the Revolution, "often hanging them out of hand." (I recall when Walter Winchell, the late controversial columnist, was anticipating the birth of a grandchild. He said, "If it's a girl she'll be named Sue Winchell; if it's a boy it will be Lynch Winchell.")

We were already aware of the origin of Marxian, along with Quisling, Goldwynism, and Stengelism (Stengelism? Why shore, that's for Casey Stengel), as well as Jonathan Swift's Lilliputians, Brobdignagians, and Yahoos. But whence come spoonerisms, mugwumps, jackanapes, and bigots? The answers are to be found in this fascinating book.

It was enlightening to learn that brouhaha, meaning up-roar and disorder (of which there is too much these days) "is very likely from the Hebrew Barauk Habba, 'blessed is he who comes.' " There are scores of biblical references with which, presumably, all of you are familiar—such as tunket. It seems this word started out as Tophet, the Old Testament name for a place where human sacrifices were made by fire. "Tophet is hell, and like hell has lost its upper case. Indeed, it has minced down from tophet to tunket. Elderly New Englanders still say 'as sure as tunket.' " Obviously, they are reluctant, admirably so, to use the shorter designation.

Didja know that philippics comes from Demosthenes' denunciations of King Philip of Macedonia? You did? Well then, suppose you try this one for size: As a stimulating dinner conversationalist you are a deipnosophist. That's because Deipnosophistai of Athens won fame for his conversational gems.

If you are challenged by big, small, lean, fat, jolly, macabre words, to say nothing of those that defy correct pronunciation, definition or derivation—by all means dip into this addictive, seductive, and wholly disarming book.

55
Style

The Elements of Style, written by William Strunk in 1918, has flourished through many editions. The most recent, published by Macmillan, contains an introduction, some revisions, and a new chapter on writing, all by E. B. White, a long-time admirer of Strunk. The book is informative, witty, concise, and is used as a ready reference by writers who have become much better known than their mentors. Its rules warn against joining independent clauses by a comma, breaking sentences in two, employing needless words, and using a succession of loose sentences.

An appealing portion of the book deals with the strength and beauty of the King James translation of the Bible. One example places George Orwell's tongue-in-cheek paraphrase of Ecclesiastes 9:11 side by side with the passage in the KJV:

"I returned, and saw under the sun, that the race is not to the swift, nor the battle to the strong, neither yet bread to the wise, nor yet riches to men of understanding, nor yet favor to men of skill; but time and chance happeneth to them all."

"Objective consideration of contemporary phenomena compels the conclusion that success or failure in competitive activities exhibits no tendency to be commensurate with innate capacity, but that a considerable element of the unpredictable must inevitably be taken into account."

Strunk demonstrates the virtue of parallel construction by quoting from the Beatitudes: "Blessed are the poor in spirit: for theirs is the kingdom of heaven. Blessed are they that mourn: for they shall be comforted. Blessed are the meek: for they shall inherit the earth. Blessed are they which do hunger and thirst after righteousness: for they shall be filled."

It is refreshing to see encomiums heaped upon the blessed word of God by experts in the field of literature. It is especially gratifying in the face of widespread criticism of the word by men and women who hold few if any qualifications either as writers or critics.

"How sweet are thy words unto my taste! Yea, sweeter than honey to my mouth" (Psalm 119:103).

56
Semantics

The ways of liberals, in the words of Alice, get curiouser and curiouser. Where the scriptures speak they do not and where the scriptures are silent they are often vociferous. What could be more curious than a recent threat by the editor of a religious journal to bring suit against a brother for producing, word for word, a pro-abortion argument advanced by one of his writers? The threatened suit smacks of casuistry inasmuch as an offer was made by the editor's lawyer to quash the suit upon receipt of $1,000. Apparently $1,000 in cold cash represented a greater deterrent than the apostle Paul's teaching on going to law with a brother (1 Cor. 6:1-8).

The aforementioned writer maintains that abortion is not murder because there is no soul in the fetus until it is actually born and breathes in the breath of life. Elizabeth thought otherwise. When she saw Mary she was immediately filled with the Holy Spirit, saying " . . . Whence is this to me, that the *mother of my Lord* should come unto me?" (See Luke 1:35-43). Yet to this advocate of abortion, that which was in Mary was mere tissue, a blob. But to Elizabeth, who was filled with the Holy Spirit, it was her Lord.

It is true that the first man became a living soul when God breathed into his nostrils the breath of life. It is likewise true that the first man was not born; he was created, formed of the dust of the ground (Gen. 2:7). God breathed into lifeless man and he came alive; he became a living soul. As for unborn babies, they are very much alive. And as living beings they are also living souls. Hugo McCord, writing in the *Gospel Advocate*, states, "Since a baby's body is alive nine months before he is born, and since the body without the spirit is dead (James 2:26), it would follow that 'the Lord forms the spirit in man' (Zech. 12:1) the day he begins to live, nine months before birth."

Joseph Stalin had the dubious distinction of murdering a million of his own people during his career. But Stalin was a piker compared to what is going on in the U.S. About a million fetuses are being murdered each year. Be it remembered, a child by any other name is still a child. And murder is murder, even when it is called abortion.

57

"All Flesh is as Grass"

When Marie Antoinette came to share the throne of France with Louis XVI in 1774 she was, according to her biographer Stefan Zweig, "blinded by her craving for amusement; nothing but perpetual change in the round of pleasure appeased her nervous unrest." Years later, having been tried in the crucible of suffering and condemned to die, she penned a remarkably touching letter to her sister-in-law, Elisabeth. In her extremity this once giddy woman, now prematurely aged, wrote "I have just been sentenced to death. I hope to show the firmness which he (Louis) showed during his last moments." And firm she was, to the end.

The letter expressed love and concern for her children, including the nine-year-old son whose false testimony had been used against her. "I send them both my blessing, in the hope that some day they will be with you once more and will be able to enjoy your tender care." She asked Elisabeth to forgive her son, remembering "how young he is, and how easy it is to make a child say whatever one wants." Then the queen wrote, "I ask the forgiveness of all those whom I have known. I forgive my enemies the evil they have done me." She met the cruel blade on October 16, 1793. Tragically, the letter was never received by Elisabeth and she too was guillotined the following year.

The scene of Marie Antoinette's death, the Place de la Révolution, is now known as the Place de la Concorde—down which triumphant Nazis stormed more than a century later, pouring into the Champs-Élysées and thronging about the Arc de Triomphe. Thus the grim story of Louis and Marie Antoinette is but a page in the age-old account of "man's inhumanity to man." Moreover, their few friends and many enemies have been dead for a hundred fifty years.

"All flesh is as grass, and all the glory thereof as the flower of the grass. The grass withereth, and the flower falleth: but the word of the Lord abideth for ever" (1 Pet. 1:24-25).

58

Fringe Benefit

All rational people of all races and nationalities want to be happy. Yet, in spite of this innate, universal desire, happiness is little understood and infrequently achieved.

Happiness is a state of mind which, contrary to worldwide opinion, is not dependent upon wealth, health, or freedom from all manner of responsibilities. Happiness does not necessarily follow in the wake of an unbroken series of favorable experiences. All sunshine, as someone has observed, makes a desert. If Christmas were to come every morning of the year, merriment would be dissolved in dull monotony, even among little children.

With contrast there comes a greater sense of appreciation. There is, for example, the matter of a warm fire on a bitter cold day, or a cool rain shower on a broiling hot afternoon. A stunning snow capped peak looms in greater splendor when viewed from an oven-like desert floor. In early spring a crocus is incredibly beautiful blooming amid patches of ice. A rosy faced child is so very lovely when cradled in the arms of an aged man or woman—and the oldster too achieves a degree of rugged beauty.

After pain and sorrow, happiness often arrives on tip-toe—by means of a kind word or a smile, a warm handclasp or a treasured memory. Happiness and hardship are often quite compatible.

Happiness should be regarded as a fringe benefit rather than life's aim. For proof, read the beatitudes (Matt. 5:1-12) substituting the word "happy" (which is good usage) for "blessed." Many find the beatitudes extremely hard to believe. Jesus' teaching differs completely from their own ideas about happiness.

Happiness is elusive but by no stretch of imagination is it unattainable.

59

"Thou Shalt Not Steal"

When our Number 1 son was in high school he turned in his newspaper route savings for a motor scooter. He then adorned his beloved scooter with a beautiful and expensive silver horn, capable of emitting an eerie two-toned blast. The horn lasted one day. It was stolen the very first time he parked his scooter at school.

The foregoing mini tragedy, now far away and long ago, came to mind upon reading "Watch Your Hat," an essay by Jenkin Lloyd Jones on the high cost of vandalism and thievery. Actually, vandalism is a form of stealing. The writer quoted Montaigne's observation, "If rascals only understood the advantages of virtue, they would be virtuous out of sheer rascality."

Vandalism and thievery continue making their rounds day after day, leaving frustration and bitterness in their wake. The lowly mail box, designed to last a lifetime, must be replaced with tiresome regularity because of marauding vandals; the same for lawn furniture, hurricane lamps, and other decorative objects. Meantime, stores are plagued with myriads of shoplifters, many of whom are employed by the stores from whom they steal. Whether it be petty or grand larceny, embezzlement or fake bankruptcies, honest citizens are left with the bill—via higher production costs and soaring insurance rates.

The Eighth Commandment, incorporated by our Lord in His law of grace (Rom. 2:21), is given special emphasis by Paul who writes, "Let him that stole steal no more . . ." (Eph. 4:28). It is accepted, of course, that Christians will not indulge in vandalism or thievery against their fellow men; however, there is some question as to whether, on occasion, they are willing to rob God (Mal. 3:8) of time, talent and commitment—if not of money.

60

Islam

Eight hundred million people, one-fifth of the world's population, are now within the fold of Islam. Events in Iran and other oil producing Islamic countries have caused the eyes of the western world to fasten upon Muhammed's followers. To a Muslim, Islam is man's one, true religion.

Muhammed was born about 570 A.D. in the city of Mecca. According to Muhammedan belief, the prophet was 40 years of age when the angel Gabriel came to him saying, "Recite thou in the name of the Lord, who created man from clots of blood" (Koran, Sura 96). This is but one of the many conflicts between the Koran and the Bible: "Jehovah God formed man of the dust of the ground . . ." (Gen. 2:7).

Muslims are found throughout the world, including the U.S.A. In-fact, our schools are crowded with them. A recent phenomenon is seen in the Black Muslim movement. It is ironic that Muslims, who played such a cruel role in capturing and selling black Africans into slavery, are now highly regarded by some of the descendants of those very slaves. It is equally ironic that blacks who espouse Muhammedanism disdain the teachings of Christ which were responsible for the emancipation of their ancestors.

In his *Essence of the Koran*, Theodore M. R. von Keler says, "In John 16:7 we read: 'It is expedient for you that I go away; for if I go not away, the *Comforter* will not come unto you; but if I depart, I will send him unto you. And when he is come, he will reprove the world of sin, and of righteousness and of judgment.' The word *Comforter* is the English translation of the Greek word *Parakletos* used in the Greek version of the New Testament. Muhammed and his followers declare that a forgery has been made in the translation and that the real Greek word which was originally written in this verse, was *Periklutos* meaning 'the Laudable, Praised.' In Arabic these two words are translated *A'hmed* . . . equivalent to *Muhammed* in meaning. Islam, therefore, claims that Jesus himself foretold the coming of Muhammed." (p. 28).

Missionaries to Islam have found conversions to be few and far between. One man is said to have toiled in Iran for 25 years without even one convert. One reason, among many, for this incredible difficulty is that Muhammedans are horrified at the idea of Jesus being the Son of God. This, they say, cannot be because God is one. We know, of course, that Jesus prayed, "That they all may be one; as thou, Father, art in me, and I in thee . . ." (John 17:21).

Those who held Americans hostage in Iran are themselves hostages of a false religion that offers no way of escape.

61

Talents

"We hold these truths to be self-evident: That all men are created equal . . ." So said the framers of the Declaration of Independence. They were wrong. In Jesus' parable, talents were distributed "to each according to his several ability." That's the way it was then, the way it is now, and the way it will be till the end of time.

The key point in the parable is inescapable: We are responsible for the manner in which talents are used, not for the amount in our possession. In short, worth is not calculated in terms of ability but rather by the use of that ability.

The one talent man was not expected to make five more, or even two. His severe punishment came about when he refused even to try to use what he had. Obviously, ratings in heaven are decided on effort, not on potential or opportunity.

We all know what we would do with the other person's wealth. Too often, however, we are uncertain as to what should be done with the actual amount in our possession. And what about our store of Bible knowledge? is it to be buried or used? how alleviate stresses and strains that beset those about us? how be a good neighbor (in keeping with another famous parable of our Lord)? and how utilize fully our intellectual and physical skills for the betterment of others?

Heaven undoubtedly will be populated by those who on earth were millionaires and paupers, industrialists and day laborers, educated and uneducated. Their unalloyed joy will have come about because of the use that was made of God-given talents, whether great or small. This does not suggest salvation by works but rather the fulfillment of God's specific requirements as to the use of individual gifts. As for the tenants of hell, the same categories will exist. The dreadful state of the lost will have come about because of failure to put talents to proper use.

To use or not to use, that is the question. To enter the joy of the Lord or not to enter, that is the answer (Matt. 25:14-30).

Frightening isn't it?

62
Noblesse Oblige

The title of this essay has to do with ordinary obligations, including honorable conduct. Thoughtful people are aware of certain social, moral and spiritual laws without which there can be no genuine freedom. The Golden Rule states, "All things therefore whatsoever ye would that men should do unto you, even so do ye also unto them . . ." Would that those who throw cans and bottles on highways and private property and those who bash fenders in parking lots and drive off without leaving a note, as well as those who engage in vandalism and violence, might observe the rule laid down by our Lord.

The awesome capability of the computer to store vast amounts of information, which it can produce instantaneously, is a source of wonder to most of us. Yet a computer cannot understand, as human beings understand, even the simplest bit of the information it holds. How absurd for man, who is capable of understanding, to engage in courses of action for which he assumes no more responsibility than an automaton.

A widely heralded television play depicted experiences of a man and woman dying of cancer. The play could have emphasized the power and beauty of the human spirit. Instead, it glorified an adulterous relationship, thus abetting the widely accepted belief that anything is permissible among consenting adults.

Gregory, back in the sixth century, listed the seven deadly sins in this order: pride, envy, anger, sloth, avarice, gluttony

74

and lust. Not one of these violates our nation's criminal code. Obviously, there is much that is allowable in human conduct, by human beings themselves, that is contrary to the will of God. In a letter addressed to the church in a city enslaved by sin, the apostle Paul wrote "Where the Spirit of the Lord is, there is liberty" (2 Cor. 3:17). And it was the apostle Peter who insisted that Christians must not be found using their freedom (liberty) "For a cloak of wickedness" (1 Pet. 2:16).

63
Morning Mood

It is six o'clock in the morning. Another hour will pass before the sun climbs over the hill to send its beams in my window. Households are coming alive all over the city—with many a complaint about how much work needs to be done this day. Yet there is an inner awareness of the misery that would accrue if suddenly the opportunity and the joy of work should cease.

The birds have been tuning up. Now the concert begins in earnest. A soloist is heard above the symphony and presently the melody is taken up by another and still another. A squirrel nervously investigates both sides of a tree. Unable to decide which is the better position, he drops lightly to the wet grass. Peter Rabbit sits stolidly by. Except for an ear that twitches slightly one would think Brer Rabbit to be made of plaster.

But now there are other sounds that obtrude, cars whooshing by on Granny White Pike, a siren in the distance and, best of all, those wonderful kitchen sounds. There is the squeak of an oven door and, if one strains an ear, the noisy frying of bacon (heard less often in these days of soaring prices) accompanied by the tantalizing aroma of coffee.

We leave the birds and other creatures to their devices. God will feed them (Mat. 6:25) but it has been decreed that man must eat his bread by the sweat of his face (Gen. 3:19). The apostle Paul adds, ". . . If any will not work, neither let him eat" (2 Thess. 3:10).

And so another day has come, a day for honest work, and for gratitude, and the giving of thanks to the Giver of all good things, remembering that at the top of the work list for this day and every day is the divinely inspired dictum, ". . . Work out your own salvation with fear and trembling; for it is God who worketh in you both to will and to work for his good pleasure" (Phil. 2:12-13).

64

True Worth

Harry Emerson Fosdick, brilliant scholar and eloquent speaker of a past generation was, unfortunately, a liberal who discounted much that is found in the Bible. This is readily apparent to one who reads his book, *Understanding The Bible.* However, there were times when Fosdick with true insight got to the heart of certain Bible themes. A case in point is found in his famous sermon, "The Cross, an Amazing Paradox," in which he related the following story:

Muretus, in the 17th century, a fugitive from France, fell ill in Lombardy, and looking like a vagabond in rags asked aid of the doctors. The physicians discussed his case in Latin, not thinking that this bedraggled pauper could understand the learned tongue. Facismus experimentum in anima vili, they said, "Let us try an experiment with this worthless creature." And to their amazement the "worthless creature" spoke to them in Latin: Vilem animam appellas pro qua Christus non dedignatus est mori? "Will you call worthless one for whom Christ did not disdain to die?"

A brazen murderer, interviewed on television, was asked if he had any qualms or regrets about having killed a fellow man. He replied, "No, it doesn't mean a thing to me." To this man life is cheap. But life is not cheap. The Son of God, our Savior, died that all men might live (John 3:16). And it was our Savior who asked, "What shall a man be profited, if he shall gain the whole world, and forfeit his life? or what shall a man give in exchange for his life?" (Matt. 16:26).

Do we detect an air of wonder in the words of Paul? "Faithful is the saying, and worthy of all acceptation, that Christ Jesus came into the world to save sinners; of whom I am chief" (1 Tim. 1:15). ". . . the Son of God, who loved *me*, and gave himself up for *me*" (Gal. 2:20).

65

In Praise of Kind Words

"*Be kindly affectioned one to another with brotherly love.*"   —Romans 12:10

To love someone more dearly every day,
To help a wandering child to find his way,
To ponder o'er a noble thought and pray,
And smile when evening falls: This is my task.

Many informed people in our troubled land are trying, with little success, to avoid the stresses and strains that contribute greatly to mental and physical suffering. Alas, stresses and strains are here to stay.

Jim Hampton wrote some time ago, "Stress is as endemic among 20th century industrialized societies as threats from smallpox, bubonic plague, and the saber-toothed tiger were among earlier peoples. Stress wears limitless disguises. An unkind word, a social snub, a feeling of being unappreciated or worthless—all these stressors can have debilitating consequences."

Christians are called upon to "take up the whole armor of God" so as to "be able to withstand in the evil day, and, having done all, to stand" (Eph. 6:13). There are times, however, when the combatants must find relief from the fray by means of the rest and peace afforded by prayer and meditation.

Here, then, is our premise: We are weak, stumbling creatures of the dust, subject to the ills and heartaches common to mankind. Therefore it behooves us every one to ease the burdens of others whenever and wherever possible. One of the better ways of helping comes in the voicing of a few kind words of encouragement. What saith the scriptures? "Bear ye one another's burdens, and so fulfil the law of Christ" (Gal. 6:2).

66

Good Old Joe

Shortly after that diplomatic disaster, the Potsdam Agreement, President Harry S. Truman is said to have referred to Iosif Vissarionovich Dzhugashvili, alias Joseph Stalin, as "good old Joe." Complaints were raised throughout our nation since it was common knowledge that Stalin, among other misdeeds, had caused the death of a million of his own people by means of starvation, forced labor in Siberia, and outright murder. How in the name of common decency, it was asked, could anyone be so ruthless as to implement the death of a million human beings?

We have no answer nor do we have an answer for questions raised by startling statistics that appeared in *U. S. News & World Report.* There were 50,000 abortions in 1969. Then came a landmark liberal abortion law adopted by New York State in 1970. In that year the number of abortions rose to 193,500. The following year the figure was 586,800. Another landmark decision by the U. S. Supreme Court came in 1973 curtailing the right of States to ban abortions. In that year the figure rose to 745,000. In 1974 there were 900,000 abortions and now the number has risen to more than a million each year.

A million lives snuffed out in one year! If good old Joe were still around he would be jealous. The same for King Herod. It took that arch fiend Stalin about five years to do away with a million Russians. In about the same amount of time there have been five million abortions in the United States. And the figures continue to rise at a phenomenal rate.

There are five abortion clinics in my home town. Their newspaper advertisements invite calls 24 hours a day. They report 15 to 20 abortions in each clinic every week day and 25 on Saturdays. This adds up to about 215 abortions every week.

My, my, wasn't old Joe a wicked man! And aren't we above reproach!

67

Flaws

Columnist Tom Tiede, writing from (you guessed it) Washington, deals with the current political scene. He gives special attention to those who aspire to the highest office in the land and, in doing so, lists certain flaws in the makeup of Presidents of an earlier day.

"In earier America," Tiede writes, "one could be flawed and still be President. Rutherford Hayes had what was considered to be an incestuous relationship with his sister. Andrew Jackson delivered his inaugural address to Congress in a state of inebriation . . . Grover Cleveland (was the) father of an illegitimate child . . ." And now comes the blockbuster: "James Garfield, a preacher, once publicly argued against evolution!"

How bad can a man get? Imagine, a President of the United States of America, a nation founded on Bible principles and Christian belief—imagine his having such unalloyed temerity as to argue against the sacrosanct position of those who accept the high-flown, unproved theories of evolution!

How dare a President accept implicitly the opening words of the Bible which state grandly, "In the beginning God created the heavens and the earth"? How dare he insist on creationism? Above all, how dare he refuse to accept the "fact" of his origin in the primeval slime and reject such supposed ancestry as may be found in artists' drawings of Cro-Magnon, Neanderthal, Zinjanthropus, Sinanthropus, Australopithecus, etc., etc.

But then, President Garfield was a preacher. What can you expect?

68

"That Which Is Perfect"

Miracles recorded in the New Testament were temporary measures of confirmation, scaffolding utilized by the divine builder of the church. When no longer needed, the scaffolding was discarded. "When that which is perfect is come, that which is part shall be done away" (1 Cor. 13:10).

Our Lord gave gifts unto men, "some to be apostles . . . prophets . . . evangelists . . . pastors and teachers" (Eph. 4:11.) Paul says these gifts were to continue "till we all come in the unity of the faith" (Eph. 4:13)—not forever, not till judgment day, but "till we all come in the unity of the faith." The word "faith" is used frequently in the New Testament to indicate a body of truth, the new covenant. "Earnestly contend for *the faith* once delivered to the saints" (Jude 3). ". . . now preached *the faith* . . ." (Gal. 1:23).

The word "till" looks to a time of termination. "I shall read the book till I have finished." Special gifts and miracles were to continue till the coming of the complete revelation of the faith, which is to say the truth, the gospel, or the last will and testament of our Lord.

In 1 Corinthians 12:8-10 Paul catalogs spiritual gifts which include prophesy, tongues, and supernatural knowledge. In the following chapter he says prophecies, tongues and knowledge shall vanish away but faith, hope and love will abide. Only with the coming of the perfect was the imperfect to be done away.

That which is perfect has come. James writes of the "perfect law of liberty" (James 1:25). When the perfect (written) word is come, then that which is in part (miracles) shall be done away.

It is high time for those in the Lord's church who have become enamored with Pentecostalism to heed Paul's stringent warning to "be no longer children, tossed to and fro and carried about with every wind of doctrine, by the sleight of men, in craftiness, after the wiles of error" (Eph. 4:14).

69

More Than You Ever Wanted To Know About Christmas

Just about everybody knows "Christmas" means the mass of Christ, that the name is Catholic in origin, that our Lord was not born on December 25, that Santa Claus is a corruption of the Dutch for Saint Nicolas, and that St. Nick was a fuzzy character who supposedly saved three girls from a life of shame by surreptitiously providing them with dowries. According to the legend, the father of the girls would have sold them had it not been for Nick's generosity and concern. We are of the opinion that he would have been justified in taking the father by the scruff of the neck and shaking him mightily until he yelled uncle, or the Dutch equivalent thereof.

It is equally true that most everybody in America finds the Christmas season to be filled with happy times, good food, and joyful reunions. Back in the old days the ashes of the Yule log (Yule winter celebrations antedate Christianity by many centuries) were strewn over crops to prevent failure and placed in water that cows drank to make the milk pure and plentiful. We don't know why Santa's mode of entry is via the chimney unless the legend came from Amsterdam where doors and stairways are so narrow a corpulent figure would find it difficult to squeeze through. In this connection I recall my own incipient childhood doubts because our house, sans fireplace, was heated by woodburning stoves and along about Christmastime the pipes, up there in the frozen north, were usually red hot.

The custom of giving presents was, at the outset, on December 6. However, this date coincided with the orgies of the Roman saturnalia, a time sacred to Saturn when the majority of the people got drunk and acted very much like lots of people nowadays. Some wag has observed that at this season neither the past nor the future are as important as the present. We must admit that we like the present too (even better in the plural), especially when it fits, tastes good, or provides interesting reading.

Of all the customs handed down through the years, our personal preference is the greeting card. (Fie on the post office for making them so expensive to send!) Therefore, in the time honored fashion we are pleased to say, Merry Christmas, Happy holidays and much joy in the year ahead.

70

"Be Thankful Unto Him and Bless His Name"

On December 21, 1620, 102 weary Pilgrims landed at Plymouth. The voyage was an incredible feat of endurance. That frail little craft, the Mayflower, was but 90 feet long and 20 wide. And now, so they thought, the promised land was theirs.

Six months later half of them were dead. The remainder endured unbelievable hardships. Yet, at the first harvest, they set aside a day on which to give special thanks to God for their blessings. Their poverty was exceeded only by their gratitude. They heeded readily the exhortation of the Psalmist:

> Enter into his gates with thanksgiving, and into his
> courts with praise: be thankful unto him, and bless
> his name. For the Lord is good; his mercy is everlast-
> ing; and his truth endureth to all generations.

One hundred fifty-six years after the landing of the Pilgrims, "Our fathers brought forth on this continent a new nation, conceived in liberty, and dedicated to the proposition that all men are created equal." Now, in the providence of God upward of 200 additional years have rolled by—and our nation still stands.

De Toqueville once said, "America is great because she is good; when America is no longer good she will no longer be great." Never in her history has America been so close to moral disintegration. And while our government continues to be torn with dissension there are evidences of similar weakness in the church. But goodness, that ingredient absolutely essential to genuine progress, has not disappeared entirely. There is much good in government. There is great good in the church. Let us be thankful. Let us praise our heavenly

Father's holy name. Let us know that "his mercy is everlasting and his truth endureth to all generations."

71

The Fourth

Much is being said these days about the precarious state of our nation as well as the condition of the church. Dire predictions have been made of impending riot and insurrection. But just for today, let's keep it light and give a nod to nostalgia.

When I was a boy, back in the dark ages, the 4th of July was a time for the exploding of firecrackers and attendance at picnics which were featured by games, patriotic music, equally patriotic oratory, and salutes to aging Civil War veterans. The veterans occupied honored positions in front of a crowded bandstand.

Times have changed, to coin a phrase. Firecrackers are banned in most places. There are no Civil War veterans left. Patriotic music is less popular than in years gone by and patriotic oratory, especially when spiced with scripture quotations, arouses the ire of sophisticates. Incidentally, a sophisticate is defined as one who suffers "impairment or debasement, as by some change affecting purity or genuineness." So much for those who take pride in their sophistication.

Also, back in those dear, dim days, dinner on the ground (actually several feet off the ground) was a challenge to every little boy to outdo his friends in a gastronomic orgy. There was always a stunning array of ham and fried chicken, along with bowls and bowls of vegetables and mouth watering cakes and pies, together with huge buckets of lemonade. After having arisen nobly to the challenge, the youngster could be excused if a certain euphoric malaise rendered his attention span almost non-existent during the speechmaking.

The dewy eyed wonder of a little boy has been replaced by a more nature outlook. However, although we would not say with Browning that "all's right with the world," we would agree fervently that "God's in His heaven," and reasons for wonder are all about us.

72

Can Any Good Thing Come Out of Athens?

Aristides, Greek Christian of the 2nd century, wrote the *Apology of Aristides.* The complete manuscript in Syriac was found on Mt. Sinai in 1889. The *Apology,* a vindication or defense, is addressed to Caesar Titus Hadrinanus Antoninus (Hadrian) and was written upward of 1800 years ago. It deals with Barbarians, Greeks, Jews and Christians.

"The Christians . . . trace the beginning of their religion from Jesus the Messiah . . . named the Son of God Most High. And it is said that God came down from heaven and from a Hebrew virgin assumed and clothed himself with flesh; and the Son of God lived in a daughter of man. This is taught in the gospel, as it is called, which a short time ago was preached among them; and you also if you will read therein, may perceive the power which belongs to it.

"This Jesus, then, was born of the race of the Hebrews; and he had twelve disciples in order that the purpose of his incarnation might in time be accomplished. But he himself was pierced by the Jews, and he died and was buried; and they say that after three days he rose and ascended to heaven. Therefore these twelve disciples went forth throughout the known parts of the world, and kept showing his greatness with all modesty and uprightness.

"Christians, O King . . . do not commit adultery nor fornication, nor bear false witness, nor embezzle what is held in pledge, nor covet what is not theirs. They honor father and mother, and show kindness to those near to them; and whenever they are judges, they judge uprightly. They do not worship idols. . . Falsehood is not found among them; and they love one another, and from widows they do not turn away their esteem . . . they observe the precepts of their Messiah with much care, living justly and soberly as the Lord their God commanded them . . ." (*The Ante-Nicene Christian Library, Addl. Vol., pp. 259, 276-7.*)

The foregoing excerpt is a demonstration of the effectiveness of Paul's great sermon on Mars Hill. Although some mocked when they heard of the resurrection, there were others who "clave unto him, and believed." Years later Aristides was among the believers.

73

Entropy

The second law of Thermodynamics deals with entropy, the process by which the universe is running down like a clock. Anyone over sixty who spends all day Saturday working in the yard will have a working knowledge of the theory on Sunday morning.

Actually, entropy has to do with our present energy crisis, that much-discussed subject with which we are weary and on which we would welcome a moratorium. However, the crisis is a fact of life that will not go away if we close our eyes. In this connection it would be interesting to hear comments from those who long have espoused theories of evolution, theories that insist nature's processes are constantly advancing from less to greater with replacement moving at a faster rate then dissipation.

In the spiritual realm entropy's ravages will also take place—unless individuals and congregations are constantly alerted to the necessity of rebuilding. "Builded up in Him" (Col. 2:7) and "built up a spiritual house" (1 Pet. 2:5) are not empty phrases. Timothy was exhorted to "guard that . . . committed unto" him (1 Tim. 6:20) and certainly one of the purposes of the second epistle of Peter was to "stir up" sincere minds by putting them in remembrance (2 Pet. 3:1).

Perhaps Paul said it best of all: "though our outward man is decaying, yet our inward man is renewed day by day" (2 Cor. 4:16).

74

The Age of the Earth

A book written by Philip Henry Gosse, published in 1857, is entitled *Omphalos: An Attempt to Untie the Geological Knot.* Nearly a hundred years later Bernard Ramm, in *Christian View of Science and Scripture,* comments at length on the conclusions reached by Gosse.

Gosse advanced the opinion that creation "is the sudden bursting into a circle." He points out that there is no one state in all the course of existence which more than any other affords a natural starting point. The stage arbitrarily selected by God is the preternatural starting place.

Omphalos is a curious word for use in a book title. It is a Greek word meaning navel. There is an old story about how one would recognize Adam in the hereafter. Adam, according to the story, would not have a navel. But no. Gosse argues that Adam was created whole and complete in the circle of life— just as if he had gone through the entire circle—and so it was with all other matter created. For example, the trees in the garden, though created instantaneously, would be complete with age rings.

This gives rise to the matter of real time vs. ideal time. At the moment of creation Adam's actual or real time on earth was no time at all. He did not exist until the moment he was created. On the other hand, Adam's ideal time was that of a mature man, say 25 or 30 years. Presumably he had all the characteristics of maturity just as did the trees. Whereas a tree might appear to be 40 or 50 years old (ideal time), its real time when Adam appeared was to be counted only from the third day of creation.

The question arises as to how this applies to geology. This is especially interesting in the light of scientists' estimates of the age of the earth in terms of millions upon millions of years. Whereas the Bible accounts for only a few thousand years, the earth's ideal age can be thought of in terms of those millions of years claimed by science. Thus coal, oil, fossils and geologic processes indicative of great age may be thought of in terms of ideal time, not real or historical time.

We think the idea is sound. Unlike Bishop Ussher, Gosse is not attempting to set the date of creation; he is simply limiting the wild guesses of science.

75

"The Firm Foundation of God Standeth"

"With malice toward none, with charity for all, with firmness in the right as God gives us to see the right, let us strive on to finish the work we are in . . ." These familiar words, from Lincoln's Second Inaugural Address, have a ring of sincerity that transcends the sham with which political utterances are sometimes infused. One month following his address the President was dead, victim of an assassin whose malice, lack of charity, and inability to see the right, allowed him to carry out his infamous scheme.

Now, more than a hundred years later, a battle of words is being waged in Congress, unrest and violence appear to be gaining momentum throughout the world, Arab atrocities and Israeli retaliation are commonplace, French separatists in Canada have sought unsuccessfully to withdraw from the Commonwealth, Italian terrorists continue cowardly attacks against government figures, Communist-inspired disruptions are everywhere—and so it goes. As Winston Churchill once pictured war-torn Europe, "Death stands at attention, obedient, expectant and ready to serve . . . ready to pulverize without hope of repair, what is left of civilization."

"What is left of civilization." A chilling phrase! Ordinarily we think of our era as the very zenith of civilization. The same evaluation may have occupied the thinking of the Babylonians prior to the appearance of the handwriting on the wall. As with Babylon so with the world powers that followed. Is it then so improbable that civilization as we know it will also collapse and die? What of the ponderous inverted pyramid of big government whose prodigious cost becomes greater with each passing day? What of ineffective social reforms? of national discontent? of a penchant for the pitching of tents toward Sodom? And lastly, what of threats of nuclear warfare that could blot out millions at a single stroke, leaving vast portions of earth uninhabitable for a few survivors?

Let us not be intimidated by such towering questions. Instead, let us be strengthened by the certain knowledge that righteousness still abounds. Consider this quote from the late Charles Madison Sarratt who died at the age of 89. To a class at Vanderbilt Dr. Sarratt said, "Today I am going to give you two examinations, one in trigonometry and one in honesty. I hope you will pass them both. But if you must fail one, let it be trigonometry. For there are many good men in the world today who cannot pass an examination in trigonometry." Beyond the wisdom of Dr. Sarratt is the greater wisdom of the inspired apostle Paul who exhorted, " . . . Provide things honest in the sight of all men" (Rom. 12:17).

76

On Attempting to Hide From God

"Whither shall I go from thy Spirit? Or whither shall I flee from thy presence? If I ascend up into heaven, thou art there: If I make my bed in Sheol, behold, thou art there. If I take the wings of the morning, and dwell in the uttermost parts of the sea; Even there shall thy hand lead me, and thy right hand shall hold me" (Psalm 139:7-10).

The purpose of true religion is to restore fallen man to God. Yet the history of mankind is a history of individual and collective attempts to flee from the divine Presence. In a sense, every sin that man commits is an admission that he is attempting to run away from his Creator and Protector. Neither the bluster of the infidel nor the sanctimony of the hypocrite can screen a man from the eyes of his maker.

The first man and woman tried to hide among the trees of Eden—and failed. And so it is with those who utilize the elaborate trappings provided by modern society. There is no place in time or space where man may elude the watchful eye of God. "The eyes of Jehovah are in every place, keeping watch upon the evil and the good" (Prov. 15:3).

We are living in the age of The Bomb. Scientist and lay-men alike are now aware of the insistent, inescapable fact that there is no place to hide. Within the atom lies a power which, if used in anger, could bring death and devastation to great cities the world over. And yet, the combined power of every nuclear device in the world is in no way comparable to the Power that created the atom. That One who marks the fall of a tiny, insignificant sparrow knows well our hearts and hopes. The entire universe in his His hand. That includes you. It includes me.

77

". . . from everlasting to everlasting, thou art God"

John Alfred Brashear was reared in poverty and his formal education ended in the sixth grade. Yet this handicap did not keep him from becoming one of the great scientists of his day. Long hours of study and application enabled him to rise above his poor prospects. He and his beloved wife often walked arm in arm at night; leaving the poor district in which they lived they would study the stars from the summit of a nearby hill. A single stone marking their graves bears the inscription, "We have loved the stars, we are not afraid of the night." The Brashears were fascinated by the mystery of an illimitable universe.

Light, as you know, travels at a speed of 186,000 miles per second. How far does it travel in the 3600 seconds that make an hour? And how many seconds in a year? A light year, the distance light travels in one year, is 588 septillion miles. Add to this the fact that our galaxy is 100,000 or so light years across that is to say, 100,000 times 588 septillion miles. Before bogging down, let us consider the 2½ million galaxies glibly referred to by astronomers, each of which contains some 100 billion stars. Oh yes, while contemplating space travel beyond the sun and moon to the nearest star outside our galaxy, ponder the fact that it's about ¾ of a million light years away. There is much ado these days about UFO visitations to earth from outer space, so be it remembered that it would take a radio wave well over a million years to reach that nearby galaxy.

In a day in which the majestic power of God is subjected to cheap jokes and ridicule, may we in awe take to heart the words of the Psalmist: "O Lord our Lord, how excellent is thy name in all the earth! who hast set thy glory above the heavens. When I consider thy heavens, the work of thy fingers, the moon and the stars, which thou hast ordained; What is man, that thou art mindful of him?" "The heavens declare the glory of God; and the firmament showeth his handiwork." (Psalm 8:1, 3, 4; 19:1).

While we're at it, let us go back to the key to all existence: "In the beginning God created the heavens and the earth" (Gen. 1:1).

78
Easy Landing

Go back with me to that time in the not-too-distant past when the ultimate in air travel was a DC-3 on which, wonder of luxurious wonders, a sumptuous meal was served—consisting usually of a dry sandwich and coke or coffee. In those early days a brisk travelogue was often narrated by the pilot. Because the planes were not adequately pressurized, several days were required for one's ears to become unstopped. And woe to that one who braved a flight while nursing a cold.

We shall never forget a flight during which a motor stopped dead. The pilot revved up the remaining motor to maximum speed. This caused the plane to shiver violently. The shaking increased until it was almost equal to the shaking of the passengers. Meantime, our loquacious pilot was strangely silent. For some reason he had lost interest in his travelogue—as was also the case with the passengers.

Eventually, in what seemed hours but actually was only a short time, the pilot came on the intercom and announced, "We have been in contact with Love Field. We have clearance and will go straight in. It should be an easy landing." We were a mite doubtful about making an easy landing but the pilot set it down beautifully, in spite of the way the plane shook, rattled and rolled. When we were safely on the runway wild applause and bravos filled the cabin.

On our journey from earth to heaven there are similar tense moments. We are aware, of course, that many are in trouble. Moreover, we are prompted to think long thoughts about our own safe arrival. Here, for example, is a once happy home where dissension now rules. There is a once faithful servant of the Lord who has left the church. And all about us are those who have allowed the love of the world to come between them and their God. The airport is not far away and it has a clear, golden runway, but they are destined to crash.

The journey is not complete until a safe landing has been made. Paul warns against returning to the weak and beggarly elements of bondage (Gal. 4:9). He tells of Demas who forsook him, having loved this present world (2 Tim. 4:10). John exhorts, "Love not the world," and warns of lusts of the flesh and eyes, and of destructive pride (1 John 2:15-16). As for our Lord, he admonishes, "Be thou faithful unto death, and I will give thee the crown of life" (Rev. 2:10).

It is more difficult to land safely than to take off. In World War II the kamikaze pilots deliberately destroyed themselves as they destroyed others. Christians have a mandate—to save themselves as they save others.

79
Propinquity

In the recent past the word "togetherness" was in vogue as is the word "meaningful" today. There is a surfeit of comment on meaningful relationships, meaningful worship, meaningful attitudes, ad infinitum. But today let's talk about togetherness.

Our government has sought to insure togetherness by the issuance of directives relating to housing and education. Opposition to enforced mixing of those that have neither common interests nor philosophies has been blithely ignored. For example, the original architects of that monstrous practice of wholesale busing of school-children away from their home communities have concluded the project is a total failure and should be rescinded. Yet busing is proliferating at great cost in money, school spirit, racial equanimity, and peace of mind. All ethnic groups, in greater part, are weary of the farce.

As in secular matters, so in matters of the spirit. There are some who would have the church forsake her doctrinal purity in the interest of "spiritual togetherness." Never mind the false doctrines espoused by various ones, they seem to be saying, the important thing is getting together and opting for peace. But peace at any price is wrong. Besides, peace on the spiritual front cannot be gained by lumping together widely differing beliefs in the name of brotherhood, any more than peace can be legislated by enforced disruption of families and neighborhood boundaries.

The apostle Paul's inspired directive must be heeded above all man-made schemes for unity: ". . . Let us walk by the same rule, let us mind the same thing" (Phil. 3:16). Yea and verily, David said it is good "for brethren to dwell together in unity." However, in spite of teaching to the contrary, it is extremely important that a definite determination be made as to what constitutes brotherhood. Those who would "keep the unity of the Spirit in the bond of peace" must accept the fact that "there is one body, and one Spirit, even as also ye were called in one hope of your calling; one Lord, and one faith, one baptism, one God and Father of all, who is over all, and through all, and in all" (Eph. 4:3-6).

94

80
The Real Issue

"A sin takes on new and real terrors when there seems a chance that it is going to be found out." So said Mark Twain who also said, "Man is the only animal that blushes. Or needs to."

If Mark were still around he would find it takes some doing these days to make a man blush. This, of course, is not to say there is no longer any need for blushing. Though the need remains, the blush has almost gone the way of the dodo. Situations that once caused faces to redden are still here but we have become hardened. For proof tune in a talk show, any talk show.

To some extent we are all influenced by the speech and actions of others. We find ourselves ensnared by speech patterns and fashions. When men's jackets were introduced with ridiculously wide lapels, many said they would never wear them—but they did. (I'm afraid to comment on women's apparel). We are somewhat like the caterpillar who said, while watching a butterfly, "You'll never get me in an outfit like that."

As for speech patterns, those who once cringed when the word *like* was inserted needlessly in a sentence, often find they are doing some inserting themselves. "*Like* I was going to town." The same for *you know*. "*Like* I was going to town, *you know? like* my car broke down, *you know? like* I should have taken the bus, *you know?*"

The foregoing however, is something less than fatal. Speech patterns are subject to change. We trust the change will be for the better. This is not the real issue. The real issue has to do with one's manner of life in the light of God's revelation to man. And this gets us back to our starting point. No matter how you look at it, sin is not funny. Also, one's inability to blush because of a seared conscience (1 Tim. 4:2) is not impressive. The Christian is responsive as well as responsible. Time *was* when Israel unashamedly worshipped a golden calf (Ex. 32:25). Time *is* when spiritual Israel must glory unashamedly in the gospel, knowing assuredly that the righteous live by faith (Rom. 1:16-17).

81
Life and Death

Napoleon often referred to fallen soldiers as having had "a good death." It seems this mass murderer preferred having his men die bravely (albeit uselessly) rather than to live (in his judgment) as cowards. However, the familiar palindrome attributed to the Corsican, "Able was I ere I saw Elba," suggests his own death, so near at hand, was not to be in the classic mold.

Nearly a hundred years after Napoleon's death, Sir William Osler, whose teaching and personality so strongly influenced medical progress, spoke in behalf of a need for the maintenance in death of human dignity. His remarks were misconstrued and he was accused of advocating euthanasia. As he neared the end of the road Osler said, "Hanging over the head of 22 million Americans over 65 is this sword of a shell of life robbed of its quality."

The writings of Elizabeth Kubler-Ross, together with charges aired in the press about alleged maleficence in nursing homes, have alerted the public as to problems encountered by the elderly. Some have elected to carry cards in billfold or purse requesting in the event of "any prolonged unconsciousness, whether due to accident, heart attack, or stroke," that nature "be allowed to take its course without benefit of an intensive care or resuscitation ward."

It is only natural that thoughtful people should consider the merits of a good death. But the matter of a good life, in terms of a priceless, eternal soul, is infinitely greater in importance. Our brief span on earth is many times that of an insect whose life cycle is but a day. On the other hand, whether we live to be thirty or a hundred and thirty, earthly life is but for a moment. "What is your life? For ye are a vapor that appeareth for a little time, and then vanisheth away" (James 4:14). As for quality. Paul tells us "Each man's work shall be made manifest: for the day shall declare it, because it is revealed in fire; and the fire itself shall prove each man's work of what sort it is" (1 Cor. 3:13).

82
"Spirits Made Perfect"

Some years ago, when debating was an approved method of seeking truth, members of the Lord's church were challenged quite often by those who subscribed to the doctrine of soul-sleeping. Advocates of the doctrine believed that the soul knows nothing when the body is dead. Their favorite passage, supposedly proving the theory, is found in Ecclesiastes 9:5, "The dead know not anything." But the passage refers to the body, including that marvelous device known as the brain. As for the soul or spirit, words often used interchangeably in the Bible, the same inspired writer says, "The dust returneth to the earth as it was, and the spirit returneth unto God who gave it" (Eccles. 12:7).

There are numerous passages that offer proof of the soul's indistructibility. There is for example, the account of the living souls of the martyrs (Rev. 6:9-11). These martyrs had died for Christ; their souls lived on.

We know very little of conditions governing the spirit world. One who actually visited that mysterious realm was forbidden to describe it (2 Cor. 12:4).

In the Old Testament, which is thought to be less clear than the New regarding matters of the spirit, we find David saying of his dead son, ". . . I shall go to him but he will not return to me" (2 Sam. 12:23). David believed in life after death.

Upon the deaths of Lazarus and the rich man a conversation took place between Abraham and the former rich man who was now in anguish. In the spirit world the power of speech is not dependent upon tongue and larynx. Of special significance is Abraham's knowledge of persons who appeared on earth (Moses and the prophets) many hundreds of years after Abraham's body had returned to dust (Luke 16:29-31). The passage highlights three matters of importance: 1) There is conscious life after death, 2) memory and recognition persist, and 3) there is a compartmentalization whereby the horror of suffering in one place is separate from joy and happiness in another.

The soul is that portion of man that is eternal. In his account of the judgment our Lord said, "These shall go away into eternal punishment: but the righteous into eternal life" (Matt. 25:46).

> "The stars shine over the earth,
> The stars shine over the sea;
> The stars look up to the mighty God,
> The stars look down on me;
> The stars may live for a million years,
> A million years and a day,
> Yet saints with God will live and love
> When the Stars have passed away."

83

"Where Shall the Ungodly and Sinner Appear?"

The perceptive and erudite Vermont Royster tells of a miscarriage of justice despite an abundance of damaging evidence against the accused. There was, in the case he describes, a supposed violation of the defendant's right to a fair trial under the Fourth Amendment which, as you know, prohibits unreasonable search and seizure.

So what happened? An informant notified the Bureau of Narcotics that a sale of heroin, that mind-destroying narcotic, would occur at a certain time and place. It did take place, precisely on schedule, and the culprit was apprehended. But the evidence, the validity of which was not questioned, was disallowed because (believe this if you can) the informant "was not a person of known reliability."

Not long ago the Chief of Police in our city expressed deep concern because of the ease with which criminals are escaping punishment. This is a familiar story. Thoughtful people, many of them victims of criminal assault, are weary of seeing hardened criminals released time and again because of absurd technicalities. It was the noted jurist William Blackstone who said, "There can be no law apart from punishment."

Strangely enough, there are those who would equate God's sure justice with the many weak decisions reached in courts throughout the nation. Those who labor under this misapprehension would do well to look at the divine record. Paul tells us that those who do not obey the gospel of our Lord "shall suffer punishment, even eternal destruction from the face of the Lord and from the glory of his might" (2 Thess. 1:9). Then there is the account of the King who one day will say to the disobedient, "Depart from me, ye cursed, into the eternal fire which is prepared for the devil and his angels" (Matt. 25:41). In the Great Commission our Lord warns bluntly that "he that disbelieveth shall be condemned." Finally, in his description of last things, John says, "Death and Hades were cast into the lake of fire. This is the second death, even the lake of fire" (Rev. 20:14).

Truly, "it is a fearful thing to fall into the hands of the living God" (Heb. 10:31). The all-encompassing question posed by the apostle Peter demands the most solemn consideration and concern of every responsible being: "If the righteous is scarcely saved, where shall the ungodly and sinner appear?" (1 Pet. 4:18).

84
Diana Singing, Past and Present

As travel agents are fond of saying, "Getting there is half the fun." Getting to the site of Diana Singing is not only fun, it's an accomplishment.

The last time Milady and I attended, after a late start, we tooled down I-65 at the sedate federally stipulated, and sometimes locally enforced, 55 MPH, or thereabout; certainly not much faster—maybe 70 or 75. Eventually we found the sylvan spot, nestled in the hills near Pulaski. Cars, trucks and campers appeared to be inextricably and hopelessly wedged in parking spaces that had been dreamed up by someone with a macabre sense of humor.

First impressions came via olfactory equipment as a tantalizing aroma of frying ham was wafted gently on the breeze. Since we had left home with nary a bite, all thoughts of singing were dissipated in favor of a desire to chomp on a greasy and voluptuous ham sandwich, or two, or three. There was no need of hurrying to add our pear-shaped tones to the sound of music inasmuch as the soiree, as advertised, was to continue throughout the night.

The people, a jillion or so, were in a festive mood. Eventually, we found our way to the auditorium, which reminded us of a shed, which it was. And there, mirabile dictu, we found two vacant seats. The jovial impresario Tom Holland was speaking. He was in rare form. Then followed a succession of muscle throated song leaders who, obviously, were enamored with certain adagio tempi. Whereas Damon had Pythias and Gilbert had Sullivan, at Diana Singing it was equally clear that Stamps-Baxter had the song leaders.

To the uninitiated, those intricate opera (I trust opera is the plural of opus) have provided those who are musically uninhibited with songs in four-part harmony that delegate equal time to all, from shrill soprano to growling bass. The melody flits back and forth while the harmony takes fanciful sorties out to the pasture, around the lake, through the woods to grandmother's house, and thence to the barn and back.

This scribe was amazed that so many songs he had neither seen nor heard before were familiar to most of the others—who sang with gusto, unbounded enthusiasm, and with a degree of decibels designed, surely, to set up a permanent ringing in one's ears.

The annual Diana Singing, deep in the heart of Middle Tennessee, is overwhelming and should be experienced at least once in a lifetime by every person capable of carrying a tune.

85

Reflections on a Night at the Opry

I remember well that cold, rainy evening when Lady Claire and I were handed a couple of Grand Ole Opry tickets. Shortly thereafter we were off and running. A portrait of G. Washington gained us entrance to the gigantic parking lot. We left the car and plunged immediately into a sea of Opry buffs intent on finding shelter. In this surging mass we witnessed end runs, cross overs and off tackle maneuvers that would have brought a smile to the dour mug of Tom Landry. At the door an usher looked at our tickets and pointed toward heaven. In spite of a severe case of acrophobia we began to climb. Somewhere in the stratosphere another helpful usher looked at our ticket stubs. He too pointed heavenward. Our climb ended on the topmost row. I looked fearlessly at the stage far below—with one eye. Sir Edmund Hillary would have been proud of me.

The performers (surely all of them were midgets) sauntered out on the stage. The Duke of Paducah regaled us with some highly improbable tales. Roy Acuff sang and balanced a bow on his chin. Loretta Lynn's appearance evoked a storm of applause. A group called the Cajun something or other played in an unbelievably fast tempo. The drummer's antics were described by the MC as "lookin' like a feller akillin' snakes." An apt description. There were no audiological difficulties. The progression of decibels was loud, louder, and unbearable. The regulars knew every song, most of which had to do with alienation of affection, incarceration, loneliness, and other cheerful themes.

When the last note had died away we descended slowly and carefully from our lofty aerie. Outside a cold wind was rising and a colder rain was falling—horizontally. Our trusty

Pontiac had disappeared. We searched. The deluge worsened. There were great splashings and horn blowings (expletives deleted). Then, oh lovely sight, the car! During the next few minutes we lived dangerously. With great skill we escaped from the parking lot unscathed. Our hearts resumed beating.

The foregoing, admittedly tinged with a modicum of hyperbole, is full proof that people will endure all manner of discomfort and hardship when engaged in activities dear to their hearts. Enthusiasm and dedication unfailingly enable us to rise above obstacles, regardless of size and power. Fortunately, these qualities work equally well or better in the Lord's church. Aye, there's the rub. Would that more people loved the Lord and His cause as they love various worldly endeavors. Conditions then would never get too hot, cold, wet, dry, troublesome, hard, or dangerous to serve Him. We recall the words of a man who is thought by many to have been a fanatic. If this be so, we need more fanatics. "I can do all things," he said, "in him that strengtheneth me" (Phil. 4:13).